COMMUNITY DEVELOPMENT FOR KINGDOM IMPACT

Helping People from Here to Eternity

J. Jeffrey Palmer

Published by private funding.

For more information and to share your thoughts on Community Development for Kingdom Impact, visit our blogsite at: https://gobgr.org/blog/

Table of Contents

Introduction

A few years ago, I wrote three short books regarding human needs ministries and their place in a modern day mission strategy. They were basically descriptive or "how to" books for those interested in using relief and development strategies. In particular, they were about community development principles as a strategy to gain access to communities, demonstrate Christ-like compassion, and use that access and compassion to initiate a transformational movement among the members of that community. The material was largely drawn from my experiences of working in Asia for over 20 years in the community development and church planting fields. It also reflected significant lessons learned from amazing people with whom I worked during those same years.

The first book, *Kingdom Development: A Compassion for People and a Passion for Souls*, primarily addressed the fact that as followers of Christ, our community development efforts can indeed be "Kingdom" development. In other words, when we holistically go to the community with the desire to effect change by addressing physical issues, we can also do it as ambassadors of Christ. By working through the community development process, we can in essence come alongside people and communities at the point of their deepest needs. We demonstrate the love of Christ as well as speak truth into their lives. There is no separation of proclamation and demonstration of the gospel. When done correctly, our good deeds validate the gospel and our sharing of truth brings the opportunity of eternal change or transformation in the lives of those receiving the message.

In the second book, *Poverty and the Kingdom of God: What in the World is God Doing Among the Poor?*, I attempted to help the reader understand the biblical definition and basis of poverty. I also wanted to show that viewing poverty through our own cultural lenses can be a dangerous thing and leads us to address poverty and the poor in a way that causes harm to both us and them. The point was that a healthy and correct biblical view of poverty is essential to anyone wanting to address it in the community, especially as a missional strategy.

In my third book, *Kingdom Communities: Koinonea as if it Really Mattered*, I wanted to give a clear step-by-step process and corresponding toolbox to those interested in attempting to practice community development. I briefly discussed the concept of community in the Bible and explored models. The majority of the book was devoted to practical community development tools for those wanting to engage the community cross culturally.

So Why Write Yet Another Book?

First of all, some people have asked for a compilation of all of the above ideas and information in one central place. This new book that you are holding is an attempt to do just that. It is a distillation of the three previous books but in actuality more of a synthesis of the first and third.

Secondly, I would like to incorporate a number of new lessons I have learned regarding community development. Community development is as much an art as it is a science. With each new community entered, the development process is implemented, and usually something new is learned. I hope to capture many of these new lessons and experiences in this book in a way that helps all of us in Kingdom community work.

Thirdly, I have learned, practiced, and gleaned new results with additional community development tools. For those who have read *Kingdom Communities*, you will note that I have combined ideas and the community development cycle has been somewhat shortened. I have also incorporated some new handy tools as well as observations of strengths and weaknesses of each tool.

Fourthly, I am adding documentation by giving practical examples of some current stories and models where Kingdom impact through community development is taking place as well as the results. I also am adding some additional lessons learned based upon field experiences and sharing some practical, useable tools for evangelism and church planting.

I will discuss some of the topics already covered in the first three books and elaborate on them a bit more. I will also be looking at some new topics as well. My hope is to capture in this one book a more comprehensive and practical way for the reader to get involved in or obtain more tools for the work of community development in God's Kingdom.

My Intended Audience

While community development is a timely and trendy topic in the United States, especially in urban renewal circles, I want to clarify that this book is primarily written for those interested in community development overseas. I am writing from the perspective of community development as a tool for missions and engaging individuals and ultimately communities for Christ.

I am also writing from an experiential as well as professional level. I believe that good community development done well with the best tools and training available can be and is a valid way to express the gospel in deed (demonstration), leading to strategic opportunities for proclamation.

It will become clear that most of my experience and work comes from extremely poor, rural communities and people groups. I have little experience with urban community development and I am the first to admit my shortcomings in this particular area. I do have confidence that the principles and tools of community development discussed in this book potentially have broad applications across differing communities.

About the Structure of This Book

This book basically has two sections. The first three chapters deal with the biblical and missiological implications of community development and working with the poor. They attempt to lay a solid foundation for the "what" and "why" of utilizing community development as a missions strategy. It is written for those wanting to go deeper with regard to the spiritual/missions aspect of the topic.

The second section (chapter 4 and following) deals more with the practical application of the community development process. It walks through the process and looks at tools in each step. Both are essential to achieve the intended Kingdom impact on communities.

A Word About the Title

A few who have already previewed this book have asked about the title. They understand the "Community Development for Kingdom Impact" part. It's the sub-title, "Helping People from Here to Eternity," that raises the question.

My hope is that through your reading of this book, you will see how the discipline of community development fits into a Kingdom impacting, missional strategy role for reaching a lost world for Christ. The basic assumption from the beginning until the end is that God created everything with a purpose. Moreover, He created us for wholeness with Him and living an abundant life according to His plan and His purposes.

When we help people and communities through the discipline of community development and we do it with a Kingdom strategy focus, we help them discover and participate in the divine nature and plan of God for their lives and their communities here on earth. We lead them to find life as God meant it to be. Additionally, if we truly do community development with a Kingdom focus, we point and lead people to life eternal that is the fulfillment of all of what He desires our lives to be.

Jesus taught His disciples to pray to God the Father, "Your Kingdom come, Your will be done on earth as it is in heaven." (Matthew 6:10) Our strategies with community development can help us show God's plan for their lives both for today "here on earth" and for eternity "as it is in heaven" – thus, from here to eternity.

I invite you to join me in this exciting journey of looking into God's Word concerning the subject of community development as a missional strategy. My hope is that you will see the practical application of the discipline, hear stories of how God has used the strategy, and then begin to apply some of the things you learn. I invite you to join me as we seek God's purpose for community not only here on earth but for all of eternity. My prayer is that this book will help motivate all of us to see "His Kingdom come and His will be done on earth as it is in heaven."

Chapter 1
Community in God's Kingdom as a Missional Strategy

What is community development? How does it fit into a global missions strategy? Why would we even have a focus on community as a missions strategy? Is not missions simply telling as many people as possible about Jesus and getting them to group as churches? We know that faith comes from hearing and hearing by the message of the cross. We also know that, in general, it is individuals who come to faith - not whole groups at one time. Hence, why community?

First, the concept of community has a special place in the heart of God. Gerald Mays says, "We were created in love, by love, and for love." I would paraphrase this by saying, "We were created in community, by community, and for community." There are no "stand alone" followers of Jesus Christ. For, as we will see, God Himself is the perfect example and author of community. He created us for an amazing union and oneness with Himself but also in a way that places us into community here and now. Furthermore, He is preparing us for an eternal community with Him. We need community; it is God's nature and our nature.

Second, a majority of the people groups with whom we are called to share the gospel are much more community oriented than our individualistic western societies. The way of community is more familiar to them than our celebration of individualism. Community is not only a cultural norm of many of the unreached but moreover a functional and practical way of life that has resulted from years of experience.

Third, communities or "groups" within communities are natural avenues to church. When we find those natural groups relating to one another, inroads for transformation and the gospel to flow can do so along pre-existing lines. Already formed groups along the lines of oikos (household), extended family, tribe, etc., can facilitate the flow and formation of Kingdom groups.

Fourth, the days of easy access and receptive groups to the advance of missions is quickly coming to a close. The remaining "unreached" and "unengaged" people and people groups are not reached and not engaged for a good reason. They live in some of the hardest to get to areas. They live in areas of open armed conflict, extreme poverty, and remoteness. They live in areas that literally beg for help in feeding their children, finding income for their families, and solving the myriad of problems assaulting their communities. Community development is an appropriate tool to address these needs.

Defining Community Development

Community development is a process by which a community is strengthened in order to creatively help meet its own needs: physical, spiritual, mental, psychological, social, economic, and political. It works from the premise that all people are equally created by God and have the basic right to food, shelter, health care, rest, education, job opportunities, and security without being excluded from or exploited by the forces of society as a whole. (O'Gorman, 1992)

A community is defined as the "we" people or the insiders. It has social interaction that is personal, spontaneous, and familiar as is commonly found in villages and smaller segments of larger populations. Since community has common ties, the members feel that they belong together either along family lines, ethno-linguistically, socially, or simply bound together by common interests. There is usually some type of territorial or geographical basis for community, but not always (e.g. an extended family unit). Generally speaking, the more isolated and remote a group is from other people, the stronger the ties and interdependency and thus the feelings of "community."

All communities, just like all individuals, undergo development. This happens whether or not an outsider such as an individual or organization helps to facilitate it. To assume that we as community development workers are the bearers of development is a false assumption. Outsiders, intent on helping local development, can be detrimental, neutral, or at best facilitators of the development potential in a given community. Our goal and aim as development workers should be as learners and then facilitators in the lives of those undergoing development. The rest is a product of the process. Development imposed from the outside is not necessarily true development or transformational.

Given that communities and their composition as well as their problems are complex, it is necessary that an integrated approach to local development is utilized. Good community development recognizes the indigenous knowledge and innate abilities of local communities to develop and thus is at its core a highly participatory methodology. It holds that people should be the principal decision makers on matters of their own problems, challenges, and resources. It mandates participation, mutual respect, and active involvement of the community if it is to be true community development. A deeper discussion on the process of community development will be conducted later in chapter 5.

What Community Development Is and What It Is Not

Community development is insiders of a community working together to solve their own problems. It is not the outsider experts providing all the answers. Too often we want to arrive in the community with expertise, resources, and technology and solve all the problems of a community. However, as we tell our development workers, the community does not need you to be their savior. They already have one, and His name is Jesus. They need you to come alongside them and participate with them in the development process.

Community development is people working together for the common good. It is not individual entrepreneurs excelling. Good community development is fair and just and lifts the whole community, not just a few. In years past, we would approach communities with the idea of finding a champion such as a model farmer who would be the implementer of the first project in the target community. The idea was that as this person/family succeeded, others would see the benefit of the introduced technology and join in. While this tends to work in an individualistic-oriented society, we have not found it to be as successful in community-oriented groups. Bringing the community along as a whole in the development process tends to allow a more sustainable development and doesn't single out one or two people/families as success stories.

Community development is more about building the software than the hardware. It is about building attitudes in the community such as confidence that the community can take charge of its future. It is about building capabilities and capacities in the community whereby the members can take on larger and larger problems. It is about building a better community, one based on biblical values, where the community becomes what God intends. And it is about building character, Christ-like character, in the people of the community. It is not just about building schools, water wells, roads, health care clinics, etc., even though these things can come out of a good community development program. It is more about what happens in the hearts of the individuals and communities as a whole that makes good community development.

In addition, good community development with a Kingdom focus is a reflection and a fruit of the gospel transforming lives individually and then collectively.

A Side Note on Development

When we talk about development in the context of this book, we will be discussing development as a core value of good, sustainable growth. The word "development" in itself implies growth. But growth for the sake of growth itself is not always necessarily good. For example, the growth of a cancer cell is an abnormal growth with the end result often concluding in the death of its original host.

We will assume, when we use this term, the positive side of development. The actual word comes from the Latin *dis* meaning "a reversal; to undo" and *voloper* meaning "to wrap up." Thus when we use the term "development" in reference to community development, we refer to an effort to help the local people, the community, to "unwrap" their potential and capacities for solving the problems that face them today as well as those problems to come in the future.

Community Development and the Kingdom of God

Community development is not a uniquely Christian discipline. There are a score of secular groups and organizations working for development and focusing on the community approach. Most of the tools and principles we teach and use for community development in this book have a commonality with what is done in secular developmental approaches. However, community development can be an effective strategy for the church to engage their local communities as well as communities all around the world.

When we practice community development with an eternal focus, we participate in what I have coined as "Kingdom Development." The idea is not that we are artificially or by our own actions building the Kingdom of God. What it means is that through our actions, compassion, and engagement of communities struggling with issues of hunger, poverty and injustice, we are doing it in a way that helps people see a picture of life that God intends both for here and now and in eternity. This allows us to bring hope and then speak hope into the lives of people in need of development.

A favorite definition of mine for the "Kingdom of God" is from Dallas Williard's *The Divine Conspiracy*. Williard states that the Kingdom is "wherever God is acknowledged as Lord and His will is done." That being, when our efforts of community development are done with a Kingdom focus and bringing people into living life according to His principles and ultimately a relationship with God, we are affecting Kingdom impact.

We believe that it is not God's plan for people to live in hunger, poverty, and injustice. These are a result and consequence of a fallen world. Thus, when we give a cup of cold water in the name of Christ, we honor God and have the opportunity to tell the recipient about the Living Water. When we give a loaf of bread to the hungry, we are being obedient disciples and have opened a door to share about the Bread of Life.

Community in the Bible

There are many examples of community in the Bible, but there is no one word that actually means "community." The word community as we know it comes from the Latin *communitas*, which is derived from the root word *communis* or "common."

The closest word or concept found in the Bible for community stems from the Greek root word *koin*. *Koin* in its most basic meaning also means "common". The idea of this word is sharing in something with someone or having in common.

There are five words in the New Testament that contain the root *koin*. Two are adjectives (sometimes used as nouns): *koinonos* and *synkoinonos*. *Koinonos* is used ten times and *synkoinonos* four times. These two words usually apply to having communion and partaking with. Two other forms of *koin* are primarily used in the verb form: *koinoneo* and *synkoinoneo*. *Koinoneo* is found eight times in the New Testament while *synkoinoneo* is found three times. They generally refer to fellowshipping, having in common, and communicating.

The fifth form of *koin* is the one that is of particular interest. This is the noun form *koinonea*. In general, *koinonea* means "fellowship" but much more.

The word *koinonea* is used 20 times in the New Testament, and it has various definitions (as per usage). In different passages, it can mean:

1. Fellowship – This is of course the most common definition given to the word. It denotes the sharing in common and close communion for the early church. It is that which is described as the outcome of fellowship as well. It is best pictured in Acts 4:32, which says, "Now the large group of those who believed were of one heart and mind, and no one said that any of his possessions was his own, but instead they held everything in common."

2. Communion – This is a deeper level of fellowship implying a partnership and "having in common." It is the confidence to give "the right hand of fellowship" to a fellow believer as James, Peter, and John did to Paul and Barnabas (Galatians 2:9). It can mean the sharing that we have together in Jesus and the Holy Spirit but infers a deep fellowship with God brought about by the Holy Spirit in the life of believers as a result of faith. This then expresses itself in ministrations to the needy (Romans 15:26) where Paul says, "for Macedonia and Achaia were pleased to make a contribution for the poor among the saints in Jerusalem." It is also used in the sharing of our faith (Philemon 6) when Paul says, "I pray that your participation in the faith may become effective through knowing every good thing that is in us for the glory of Christ."

3. Communication – Even though used only one time in this way, the word *koinonea* can mean "to communicate." This is found in Hebrews 13:16 where the author says, "Don't neglect to do what is good

and to share, for God is pleased with such sacrifices." This implies a sharing in word and in deed and is echoed later in the book of James (James 2:14-26).

4. Contribution – This was briefly referred to in the communion section above but the word *koinonea* is expressed in the willingness of believers (individually and collectively) to make a "contribution" for those in need. As shown in Romans 15:26, the word "contribution" is used to define *koinonea*. Moreover, in 2 Corinthians 9:13, the Corinthians are extolled for their "generosity/contribution/*koinonea*" for sharing with God's people.

5. Participation/Partaking/Partnership – This final usage of the word *koinonea* in the New Testament goes to the very heart of what we are trying to accomplish in our human needs ministries and development work. It too means "having in common" but also conveys more of the picture of standing "side by side" as companions with those in need (Hebrews 10:33), such as the persecuted. It implies that we "share" in the divine nature of God (2 Peter 1:3-4), and that empowers us then to "participate" in the suffering of others. "His divine power has given us everything required for life and godliness through the knowledge of Him who called us by His own glory and goodness... so that through them you may share in the divine nature, escaping the corruption that is in the world because of evil desires." To be committed to human needs ministries means to not only "contribute" or

"give" to help those in need but also it means to become involved even to the point of "participating" in their lives and problems.

At the heart of our community development work is the participation with people in their deepest needs. This can take the form of "standing beside them" in their moments of acute needs due to natural disasters. It can also take the form of "coming alongside" people in their chronic suffering due to hunger, poverty, etc. In both cases, the key concept is "participation with."

Seven Model Communities in the Bible

There are seven biblical models of what community is supposed to be and can be. Each of these is different yet have the same things in common: fellowship, communion, communication, contribution, and participation. In reverse order as found in the Bible, they are:

1. The New Heaven and New Earth – (Revelation 21 and 22) – Here we find community as it one day will be. In fact, all of history is moving this way. Here is a community where God dwells with man and they are His people. There will be no death, no mourning, no crying, and no pain. There is no need for a temple or even a sun or moon to light the way because God's glory is there and fills the place. There is nothing impure or unclean here and there is a river of life, clear and clean, flowing from the throne of God, lined by the tree of life whose

leaves are for the healing of the nations. This is community fulfilled and is as it should and one day will be.

2. The Church – (Acts 2 and 4; 1 Peter 2:9-10) – Here we have Christ's body and His community on earth. His community is "a chosen race, a royal priesthood, a holy nation, a people for His possession." They are called so in order that they might "proclaim the praises of the One who called you out of darkness into His marvelous light." They were formerly not a people, but in Christ, have now become "God's people." They are characterized by devotion to God's teachings, fellowship with one another, communion, and prayer. They are described as having all things in common and taking care of those who have needs. They meet together daily and praise God with glad and sincere hearts. Christ is the head, and they are one in heart and in the Spirit. They are to be a model of what God desires for His people now and to come.

3. Jesus and His Disciples – (The Gospels) – During His time on earth, Jesus was laying the foundation for His church. He had intimate communion with a band of twelve men, teaching, training, and modeling for them what the Kingdom of God should look like in them and among them. The twelve were also surrounded and supported by others and were wholly devoted to learning from and learning to obey their Master.

4. The Community of Israel – (Deuteronomy 10-26) – They were

the community called to proclaim that the Lord is God and He is the one true God. They were the community called to love God with all their heart, soul and strength. They were holy, set apart, and called to be a blessing to all the peoples on earth. They were called to become a great nation and to be God's own. God would bless them and make them great and promised that "all the peoples on earth will be blessed" through them (Genesis 12:2-3).

5. The Family – (Genesis 2:20-25) – At the beginning of time, God saw that everything in the world had community except for man. No suitable helper was found for him among the rest of creation. Therefore, God formed woman from the side of man to which man (Adam) proclaimed, "This one, at last, is bone of my bone and flesh of my flesh; this one will be called 'woman,' for she was taken from man." (Genesis 2:18-25) Thus a man, in due time, will leave his birth family/community and be united to his wife, and they will become one flesh, and in essence a new community.

6. The Garden – (Genesis 2:8-17) – According to this account, it is eerily striking how similar the Garden of Eden in Genesis is with the new heaven and earth of Revelation. It was created for man and provided all the things that he would need. God placed the tree of life in the garden. The only other place we see this tree in the Bible is in the new heaven and new earth. A river flowed down the middle of the Garden (such as the one from the throne in Revelation) and man was

given dominion. God's presence was there, and He would walk in the cool of the day with Adam and talk with him in perfect communion. And there was no death, until the act of disobedience (Genesis 1-3).

7. God Himself – (Genesis 1:26) – "Then God said, 'Let Us make man in Our image, according to Our likeness." This is the perfect model for community; God Himself! God the Father, God the Son, and God the Holy Spirit. From the beginning, God is community. From creation to eternity, God desires community. His very nature is community, and He knows that the best for us is found in community - but not just any community. We are only fulfilled and made complete when we participate or "community" with Him through His Son Jesus Christ and with the body of Christ, the Church. In this, we are being prepared and made perfect for an eternity in community as God has designed and will bring about! In his profound book, *Epic*, John Eldredge, speaking on the eternal love of God, says, "How wonderful to discover that God has never been alone. He has always been Trinity – Father, Son, and Holy Spirit. God has always been a fellowship." One could say that God has always been *koinonea*, and at the very heart of God is this "common-ness" and "participation" in the lives of those He loves.

Looking at the seven models above, we see some commonalities in each. First, the central focus in each of these communities is God Himself. He is to be the most exalted being and the chief inhabitant.

The ultimate goal of "Kingdom" communities is to bring glory to their Creator God. Second, these model communities are to be lived according to God's laws and in continual praise to the chief inhabitant in order to fulfill His purpose for that community. God with His people who praise, honor, and obey Him is the way community is meant to be. It begins that way in the Garden and ends that way in the New Heaven and New Earth. In between, when God's people follow, obey, and honor Him, we catch brief glimpses of true community in the family, Israel, Christ and His disciples, and the Church.

To summarize community in relation to development work and human needs ministries, it is at the very heart of God that we find the motivation and mandate to reach out to those in need.

What a Community Development Strategy Can and Cannot Do For You

In terms of a missions strategy, there are certain things that a community development approach can and cannot do for you. First of all, to be clear, community development strategies in and of their own accord cannot evangelize, make disciples, or start churches. Simply stated, "So faith comes from what is heard, and what is heard comes through the message about Christ." (Romans 10:17)

When we do our good deeds through community development and come alongside people and their struggle with hunger, poverty, and disease, we must recognize that these "good works" alone are not sufficient for the salvation of our target group. People must hear and respond to the gospel. Our good works are to serve as reflections of the gospel and God's plan for a life or community, but they must go hand in hand with proclamation. My mentor, who was a great agricultural and church planting missionary, said it best when he said, "No one ever got saved by anyone's pea patch." (Harold Watson, personal recollections)

However, there are a number of positive things that community development strategies and approaches can do for us with regard to our missions efforts.

1. They can give us access to hard-to-access areas/people groups. More and more of the last "lost" areas of the world are synonymous with restrictive areas in terms of gospel penetration. Gaining access to the last of the lost is increasingly more difficult for those stuck in traditional mission modes. The day of obtaining missionary visas is on the decline. The areas of highest strategic priority (i.e. the 10/40 Window) have barriers in place to discourage mission/missionary presence. The shift of focus from traditional missions to a community development approach in many cases allows access to otherwise hard-to-access groups and areas. It is estimated that over two-thirds of Unreached People Groups (UPGs) live in areas with high human needs.

2. They can soften a target area. In many of the creative access areas of the world, the restrictions are due to either conflicting religious views or other socio-cultural views. Much of the world views the West as still having imperialistic leanings. A community development

approach that works truly from the perspective of helping local people and communities develop utilizing their own resources, can be a way to change perceptions of who we are as westerners and even Christians. For instance, it is not unusual to do community development work in a Muslim community and hear people say, "We didn't know that Christians were caring people."

3. It can provide a viable, long-term platform. In many cases, we can get temporary access in hard-to-access areas. The problem comes when we try to gain a long-term presence in order to ensure the continuation of gospel connection with the local people. Community development programs are generally accepted to be long term (e.g. no shorter than three to five years in a community) and thus provide ample reasons for an outsider to remain in close contact/connection with a people/area.

4. It sometimes is the only clear expression of God's love through Jesus that people will ever see. Many of the areas we traditionally target for development are dark areas – physically and spiritually. A community development project addressing HIV/AIDS will often be in an area where little contact of hope is ever felt. A community development project in a brothel/slum area may be the difference between an exploited girl or boy hearing or not hearing of the hope he/she has in Jesus. A water well in Central Asia may be the only chance that a whole village will have to taste fresh water and Living Water.

5. A community development approach can (and has been shown to) be an effective tool to place in the hands of national partners who,

in many cases, do much better development work and proclamation than expatriate workers under the same conditions.

The "ABC's" of Relief and Development Strategies

Relief and development strategies and what they can do to help us in missions has been articulated as the ABC's (Charles Fielding, 2008). While Fielding has applied his acrostic mainly to health care strategies, it can be broadened to relief and development as a whole.

A – Access to unreached (and needy groups). This is access in a way that allows us to go deep in relationship and gives an opportunity to gain a presence with an audience in need of help both physically and spiritually. It is biblically based and illustrated best in the life and journeys of the Apostle Paul and colleagues.

B – Behind closed doors. This is a deep access to relationships that allow the gospel to flow. It is access that allows us to find a safe and even inviting place in a person's life and their *oikos*. It gets us to the point where Dr. Fielding has described them (the hosts) as "leaning forward" ready to hear the story of life that we have to share. "Behind closed doors" can be in a home, a tent, or even a public area. However, it is generally a place where we can meet and share with the seeker and they hear without the fear of others seeing and passing judgment. It is described in Dr. Fielding's book as "intimate conversation."

C – Care for the needy (and church planting). As we care for the needy with actions such as benevolent ministries, health care strategies, and hunger initiatives, we demonstrate the gospel in action. We also do not neglect the proclamation of the gospel as well. We care for (demonstrate) and share (proclaim) in a seamless manner as to affect the message of the whole gospel in the lives of those to whom we are seeking to minister.

D – Disciple making. The basic command of the Great Commission is to make disciples. It is not simply to go. Anyone can go. The Kingdom Development Worker goes, ministers, and makes disciples. As Dr. Fielding says, "authentic disciples are the building blocks of church-planting movements." Furthermore, it is interesting to note that the term "disciple" was by far the most common name given to those who were followers of Jesus Christ. Our goal is to minister physically and spiritually, to see the transformation of lives by the power of God's Spirit and then to see the newly emerging disciples taking the abundant life shared with them, both physical and spiritual, and share it with others.

E – Empowering of the (local) church. The local church, as it begins to emerge, is empowered into ministry. The task of evangelism, discipleship, and ministry must be instilled in the local community of believers who emerge. From the beginning, as people come to faith, begin to form into groups, etc., they need to be taught and trained in the fact that they are now a part of the body with the same responsibilities and calling to reach the unreached.

Chapter Summary

• Community development is a process by which a community is strengthened in order to creatively help meet its own needs: physical, spiritual, mental, psychological, social, economic, and political.

• Community development is insiders of a community working together to solve their own problems. It is not the outsider experts providing all the answers.

• Community development can be an effective tool for the church to engage in their local communities as well as communities all around the world.

• There are many things that community development strategies can do for us but community development strategies in and of their own accord cannot evangelize, make disciples, or start churches.

References

O'Gorman, Frances. 1992. *Charity and Change: From Bandaid to Beacon.* World Vision, Australia.

Fielding, Charles, 2008. *Preach and Heal: A Biblical Model for Missions.* Published by the International Mission Board, Richmond, VA, USA.

Chapter 2
Reconciliation, Redemption, and Missions in a Community Development Framework

What is the goal of missions? Is it simply proclamation of the gospel to the lost of the world? Is it simply to "the ends of the earth" and then the task is complete? John Piper in his classic, *Let the Nations Be Glad*, reminds us that:

> *"Missions is not the ultimate goal of the church. Worship is. Missions exists because worship doesn't... The goal of missions is the gladness of the peoples in the greatness of God...Missions is not first and ultimate: God is...All of history is moving toward one great goal, the white-hot worship of God and his Son among all the peoples or the earth. Missions is not that goal. It is the means."*

Jesus commanded us in some of His last words to His disciples:

> *"Go, therefore, and make disciples of all nations, baptizing them in the name of the Father*

and of the Son and of the Holy Spirit, teaching them to obey everything I have commanded you. And remember, I am with you always, to the end of the age." (Matthew 28:19-20)

So, we are commanded to go and make disciples of all nations. We are also commanded to baptize them in the name of the Father, Son, and Holy Spirit and we are commanded to "teach them to obey" everything that Jesus commanded. In short, we are to point people to God and make the gospel known through our words and our deeds.

The primary command is to make disciples. Disciples are basically followers of Jesus Christ. The word disciple is the most used word in the New Testament to describe the followers of Jesus. In a few places they are called Christians. In a few others, they are called believers. But mostly they are referred to as His disciples.

The biblical word for disciple comes from the Greek word *matheytes*. It is a picture of one who sits at the feet of a teacher and learns from that teacher. However, when Jesus uses the word, we see a different picture emerging.

As Jesus was travelling along the road, someone said to Him, "I will follow you wherever You go!" To which Jesus replied, "Foxes have dens, and birds of the sky have nests, but the Son of Man has no place to lay His head." (Luke 9:57-58) To follow Jesus and be His disciple, we must be willing to leave behind our creature comforts.

Then Jesus said to another person, "Follow Me." To which the man replied, "Lord, first let me go and bury my father." But Jesus told him, "Let the dead bury their own dead, but you go and spread the news of the kingdom of God." (Luke 9:59-60) To follow Jesus and be His disciple, we must also be willing to give up our social obligations.

Then another said, "I will follow You, Lord, but first let me go and say good-bye to those at my house." But Jesus said to him, "No one who puts his hand to the plow and looks back is fit for the kingdom of God." (Luke 9:61-62) To follow Jesus and be His disciple, we must even be willing to turn our backs on our families.

Then, to deepen the cost, Jesus says, "If anyone wants to come with Me, he must deny himself, take up his cross daily, and follow Me. For whoever wants to save his life will lose it, but whoever loses his life because of Me will save it." (Luke 9:23-24) To follow Jesus and be His disciple, we must ultimately be willing to lay down our own lives for Him.

Our Ministry – Reconciliation

As followers of Christ, we have a mission in life: to make Him known to every nation, tribe, people, and language. Furthermore, according to the Apostle Paul, we have also been given a ministry – one of reconciliation. In 2 Corinthians, Paul says, "Everything is from God, who reconciled us to Himself through Christ and gave us the ministry of reconciliation: That is, in Christ, God was reconciling the world to Himself, not counting their trespasses against them, and

He has committed the message of reconciliation to us. Therefore, we are ambassadors for Christ, certain that God is appealing through us. We plead on Christ's behalf, 'Be reconciled to God.' " (2 Corinthians 5:18-20)

Thus, all we do is to be about making Him known. The ministry of reconciliation is primary in terms of man being reconciled to God through a right relationship with His Son, Jesus Christ. All other relationships in our lives should reflect that primary relationship and follow, under the Lordship of Christ, God's plan for those relationships. For in the end, at the consummation of the ages, we are moving towards a wholeness of relationship with God the Father, the Son, and the Spirit for eternity. The relationships we have here on earth are to be reflections and even training grounds for that eternal oneness with our Creator.

The Four Categories of Relationships in Need of Reconciliation

I propose that there are four categories of relationships that can and should be part of our ministry of reconciliation. Addressing any of the relationships and God's plan for that relationship can be used as a gateway to the truth of the need of man's primary relationship – a right relationship with God through His Son, Jesus. Furthermore, our right relationship in any of these areas should be fruit and reflection of God's intentions for all of mankind when those relationships are in right standing. These relationships and the reconciliation thereof are a basis for our community development strategy in missions.

1. Man to God – This is the primary and thus most important relationship that a person will ever have. All other relationships depend upon this one. How a person responds to the invitation of God to join Him in a living, vibrant relationship, will be the hinge upon which all of the other relationships will swing. Only when our primary place with God is restored in a right relationship can we begin to experience the life that we were meant to live. We refer to this as the primary and vertical relationship that all others are to be built upon.

2. Man to Man – When our hearts are right and relationship with God is where it should be, we are given a wonderful opportunity to love our fellow man unconditionally. God is leading us toward a day where we are all one. This is why God places so much stress on unity in His word. Jesus said, "By this all people will know that you are My disciples, if you have love for one another." (John 13:35) Why is it that we have so many relationship problems with our fellow man when God so desires harmony and unity? And, speaking frankly, why are some of the worst relationships between people found within the body of Christ? Since we are saved by grace, it would be Christ-like to live by grace in relationship with others. We call this, as well as the following two types of relationships, horizontal relationships.

3. Man to Creation – Humankind is a part of creation. Moreover, we are the pinnacles of God's creation. There is no part of this natural world created by God that has the soul and free choice that we as humans do. We are a unique part of the creation. The enemy would like us to think that how we treat God's creation is of no consequence. He tells us that there is abundant water, air, wildlife, and all other sorts of resources. Why conserve? Why protect? Or even more dangerous, use it up before someone else can. Excesses against the environment are a break in relationship with creation and lead to disastrous results.

Satan uses hunger, poverty, and strife to intensify already poor environmental conditions in many areas of the world. Is it not interesting to note that some of the most environmentally damaged areas are those that are the poorest? Or what about those areas with internal strife? When relationships break down within communities, it generally adversely affects the community's relationship with the environment. When the rich set their hearts on more riches, the forest reserves are clear-cut for profit. When wars break out, who has time or even the energy to think about nature? When poverty and hunger are constant companions, what priority can be given to protecting biodiversity?

4. Man to Self – When our hearts are right and our relationship is where it should be with God, we are given a wonderful opportunity to love ourselves unconditionally. When our worth and identity are in God and we spend time with Him, our "God image" is restored and refreshed, allowing us to see that in essence, we are basically worthless

creatures. We are only made worthy by the Great Lover, God Himself.

What makes a treasure a treasure? Is it not the fact that someone values it as a treasure? When we return to the love relationship with God that He desires for us, we become the treasure of His eye. What better worth could we have? To see ourselves as God sees us, in a loving relationship with Him, we are free to see ourselves rightly.

Again, we look at the ministry of reconciliation in relation to all of the above relationships. The primary message/ministry is to "be reconciled to God." However, starting with any of the four, our heart and goal is to proclaim the need and truth that every person needs a relationship with God. We work on restoring good relationships in a community development effort in order to help people see God's plan for community and ultimately to see God Himself.

God's Work – Transformation

This brings us to the topic of transformation. We all desire to see people and communities alike transformed into the fullness of God's plan for them. However, just as we have been entrusted with the ministry of reconciliation, the actual act of transformation does not belong to us. It is the act of God in an individual life or in a community.

Transformation is God's work in us to change us and conform us to the image of His Son, Jesus. It can only begin with regeneration or a "spiritual" birth into God's family. This birth can only happen with the indwelling of God's Spirit in a person's heart. All of our efforts at becoming good people or "like Christ" are in vain unless it is the power of God working that within us. Frankly, we are all sinners and are prone to and will return to that sinful nature.

When God's Spirit or "seed" enters into our heart, the process of transformation can begin. It requires submission and surrender on our part to God and His Spirit, allowing the work of transformation to take place. In both the Old and New Testaments, it is the "looking" or "beholding" of the glory of the Lord that initiates the transformation. This happened with Moses when he went into the cloud on Sinai. It was so with Jesus at the transfiguration. It was what Paul meant in 2 Corinthians 3:18 when he says, "We all, with unveiled faces, are looking as in a mirror at the glory of the Lord and are being transformed into the same image from glory to glory; this is from the Lord who is the Spirit."

So, it seems pretty simple. We come to faith in Christ and God places His Spirit in our hearts. If we yield and "behold" His glory, He works the power of transformation in our hearts and lives to be conformed to the image of His Son. When we become conformed to the image of Jesus, we are moved to see the world and respond like Jesus.

Thus, in our efforts at community development, ours is not the work of transformation but rather reconciliation. We cannot "transform" communities through our efforts; that can only come by the power and grace of God. We are called to the ministry of reconciliation, that is helping restore right relationships: Man to God, man to fellow man, man to creation, and man to himself. The power that is needed for true transformation is basically unleashed by the least of saints willing to bow the knee in prayer before the Great Transformer.

To the Lost, Last, and Least

I have found that there are three major groups of people that God has a special place for in His heart: the lost, the last, and the least.

I do not mean to imply that God does not love His children, the redeemed church. But I do see His heart as the heart of a shepherd seeking the one stray out of the hundred. I also see Him as the widow who searches frantically for that one lost coin and the father who anxiously looks every day for the return of his prodigal son (Luke 15).

It is interesting to note that the missiological term popularized by Ralph Winter years ago, *panta ta ethne* ("all nations") is found primarily in the gospel of Matthew. While the concept is found throughout the Bible, it appears in three particular passages in the last few chapters of Matthew where we are shown God's concern for:

1. The Lost – (Matthew 28:18-20) "Then Jesus came near and said to them, 'All authority has been given to Me in heaven and on earth. Go, therefore, and make disciples of all nations (*panta ta ethne*) baptizing them in the name of the Father and of the Son and of the Holy Spirit.'"

2. The Last – (Matthew 24:14) "This good news of the kingdom will be proclaimed in the world as a testimony to all nations (*panta ta*

ethne). And then the end will come."

3. The Least – (Matthew 25:31-40) "When the Son of Man comes in His glory, and all the angels with Him, then He will sit on the throne of His glory. All the nations (*panta ta ethne*) will be gathered before Him, and He will separate them one from another, just as a shepherd separates the sheep from the goats...Come you who are blessed by my Father, inherit the kingdom prepared for you...Whatever you did for the least of these brothers of Mine, you did for Me."

A Growing Trend of Relief and Development Approaches and the Strategic Link to Global Missions

In 1990, Christian mission strategist Luis Bush began to talk about a vast area of the world stretching from North Africa across the Asian continent through China. As a defined area, it was reported to have the highest levels of socio-economic challenges while at the same time the least access to the Church, Christianity, and Christian resources. Since this area was between ten and forty degrees latitude north of the equator, it became known as the 10/40 Window (Bush, 1990).

The 10/40 Window has become the strategic focus of several mission agencies. Over 75% of the world's lost live in the window. Even so, there are still relatively few people and agencies targeting this area of the world. It is typically seen as an area highly resistant to the gospel with cultural, physical, and government barriers.

• The 10/40 Window is a window of major populations. Within this window, there are more than 60 countries. About 4.5 billion of the 7 billion people on earth live in this area of the world and they comprise 90% of the unreached people groups of the world.

• The 10/40 Window is a window of major world religions. Living in the window are about 1.2 billion Muslims, 1 billion Hindus, and 600 million Buddhists. Over 1 billion people in the 10/40 Window live under the influence of communism/socialism. It has been described as a belt of spiritual darkness with most of the countries being "creative access" areas whereby different strategies must be employed in order to gain access.

• The 10/40 Window is also a window of poverty, critical human needs, and suffering. Close to 80% of the poorest of the poor in the world live there. Whereas over the last fifty years the wealthy "Christian" world has gotten wealthier, the lost have grown poorer. Not only is the 10/40 Window poor, but it also has some of the highest rates of infant mortality in the world. The 10/40 Window is an area of armed conflict as well with many of these countries experiencing on-going wars. Additionally, the 10/40 Window is a place where the development potential of women is extremely low. Over 2/3 of the world's refugees are Muslims and over 90% of those are in the 10/40 window (Myers, 1996).

The Practical Aspect of Relief
and Development strategies

In recent years, most missiologists and major mission organiza-tions have shifted their focus to unreached and unengaged people groups. Basically, a people group is the largest group through which the gospel can flow without encountering a significant barrier of un-derstanding or acceptance. Unreached People Groups (UPGs) are those that are less than 2% evangelical. Unengaged Unreached Peo-ple Groups (UUPGs) are those that have no coordinated evangelical Christian missionary presence among them (Holste, 2012).

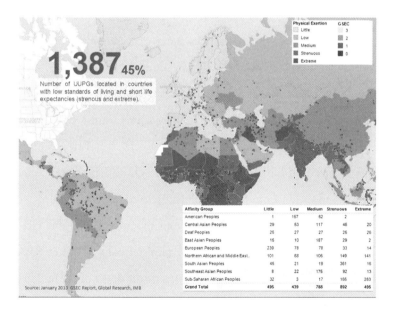

Affinity Group	Little	Low	Medium	Strenuous	Extreme
American Peoples	1	167	62	2	
Central Asian Peoples	29	63	117	46	20
Deaf Peoples	25	27	27	26	26
East Asian Peoples	16	10	187	29	2
European Peoples	239	78	78	33	14
Northern African and Middle East.	101	68	106	149	141
South Asian Peoples	45	21	19	361	16
Southeast Asian Peoples	8	22	175	92	13
Sub-Saharan African Peoples	32	3	17	166	263
Grand Total	495	439	788	892	495

When UPGs and UUPGs are mapped worldwide, they are found in various areas. However, there is a concentrated band running from

North Africa to East and Southeast Asia. This band corresponds with high levels of human suffering measured by what is called the human development index (HDI). When mapped together, it shows that 45% of unreached and unengaged groups live in areas that have strenuous to extreme human need issues (IMB Global Research, 2013). This would suggest that more than a cursory focus on relief and development strategies could be a key component to a global missions strategy. In short, the majority of the unreached and under-reached are living in areas of high human needs.

A Word on the Social Gospel

There are those in mission circles today who choose not to address any human needs due to the fear of dependency issues or the "social gospel." We teach our developmental partners not to be afraid of these concerns but to understand them as they launch into a community development strategy. For one, the gospel is social. It has everything to do with man and his condition. This is a result of the fall and consequently, separation from God manifests itself in society.

The term "social gospel" comes from the early 1900s and Hell's Kitchen, New York. A young Baptist minister named Walter Rauschenbusch desired to take the church outside the doors of the building and into the needy streets of that area. The idea was to address the issues of urban overcrowding, poor health, inequality in labor, alcoholism, etc. It was based on the theme of God's Kingdom coming (much like what we teach in community development) but due to the times and extremes, became a polarizing topic within Protestant circles, eventually leading to a more liberal interpretation of salvation and the church.

While the extremes of the social gospel led to unhealthy areas for the church, we acknowledge that the church and the Christian faith should be the best example of what society is to be and become.

Addressing Human Needs and Help That Doesn't Hurt

A few years ago, an excellent book was written by Steve Corbett and Brian Fikkert, titled *When Helping Hurts*. It was an attempt to speak to the church, especially the church in the United States, and address the issue of how to alleviate poverty without hurting those we intend to help as well as hurting ourselves. Much of it is directed at short-term volunteer trips and workers who, with good intentions, often actually cause more harm than give help when they go to other places on "mission" trips.

Corbett and Fikkert do a good job in distinguishing between relief and development. They also talk about an often hidden (to ourselves) problem called paternalism. Paternalism is basically doing for others what they can do for themselves. It is often well-intentioned, but can leave people dependent upon others and even rob them of the motivation and joy of trying to handle their own problems. It is "help" that "hurts" and leads to stunted or handicapped growth of people.

They cite various forms of paternalism as being:

1. Resource Paternalism – This stems from our "have" and "have not" philosophy of poverty. If we see the poor of the world as lacking things, the temptation is to provide them with "things" or resources. This is often done with good intentions but in a way that actually cripples a community's ability to grow in development.

2. Spiritual Paternalism – When we assume the position of spiritual superiority, we often create an unhealthy communication of what the Kingdom of God is about. We should embrace other followers of Jesus as equals and recognize that the Holy Spirit can work through them in their own cultures in a more relevant way than we can as outsiders. I have been amazed over and over at the spiritual insights that I learn from national partners if I will only listen. The one thing we do is continually point them to the Word of God for direction. But we should be open to how God speaks to them (and their culture) through His Scriptures.

3. Knowledge Paternalism – All of us are guilty of this at one time or another. It is easy to assume that people are experiencing underdevelopment because they have a lack of knowledge. I learned early on to view most local people as a whole lot smarter than I am. They could live and exist in harsh environments and with limited resources that would literally kill me if I tried to duplicate what they were doing. For instance, I came to learn that even though I was a college trained agriculturalist, the Filipino farmers I worked with were much more

capable of living and existing in their conditions. They could raise a family of six on two acres of land with only a net cash flow of US $25 per month. They could feed, clothe, house, and educate their children. I came to regard them as some of the smartest people in the world. I concluded, rightfully so, that I could not do what they did with the resources at their disposal.

4. Labor Paternalism – This sometimes stems from seeing "the poor" as helpless. When we do, we assume there is nothing they can contribute to their development process. Thus, we take over not only procuring the resources for the community but also bypass the one thing that, in many cases, they have to contribute: their labor.

5. Managerial Paternalism – This type of paternalism can manifest itself in the planning and implementation steps of the community development cycle. We trust the community to identify their problems and come up with solutions. But when it comes to the implementation and monitoring of their project, we take control. Sometimes this comes from good intentions. Oftentimes, it comes from a deep-seated belief that they cannot be good managers (as evidenced by their current conditions). We must avoid this type of paternalism if we really want the community to take charge and move forward with its development.

I would venture to add a sixth type and often hidden form of paternalism known as cultural paternalism.

6. Cultural Paternalism – This is probably the most hidden and thus dangerous form of paternalism. We are all ethnocentric, believing either consciously or subconsciously that our way of doing things is "right." Generally, we succumb to this naturally because, at the core, it is who we are and how we interpret life. Our ethnocentricity makes it hard to trust others with their way of doing things. In terms of community development, it tempts us to always want to step into the process and help people/communities make the "right" decision and choices. We have to guard our hearts, motives, and actions so as not to impose our cultural understandings and choices on the people with whom we are working. One of our core principles used in training community development workers to help overcome cultural paternalism is to try and bring every question and decision back to God's way found in the Bible. This reinforces that we don't know all the answers as well as demonstrates to our community that we are people of principles and faith. It also lays a foundation for the community in the future to be people who look to God's Word for answers and not to us.

In summary, good community development works in a way to avoid all forms of paternalism. Remember that we do have things that we can contribute as outsiders. But the insiders have much more to contribute. In the end, the problems are theirs and the solutions need to be theirs as well. There may be times that we have to step in to confront or point out a harmful practice or decision. These are generally few and far between. We are participating and "coming alongside" the community in the development process. We are not completely passive but must be careful not to dominate the process.

Chapter Summary

• As followers of Christ, we have a mission in life: to make Him known to every nation, tribe, people, and language.

• In our efforts at community development, ours is not the work of transformation but rather reconciliation. We cannot "transform" communities through our efforts; that can only come by the power and grace of God. We are called to the ministry of reconciliation.

• We desire to see both people and communities transformed into the fullness of God's plan for them.

• Good community development and good ministry as a whole works in a way to avoid all forms of paternalism.

References

Bush, Luis. 1990. *The 10/40 Window, Getting to the Core of the Core.* AD 2000 & Beyond Movement. Paper presented to Lausanne II, Manila, July 1989.

Myers, Bryant L. 1996. *The New Context of World Missions.* Monrovia, Calif.: MARC Publications.

Holste, J. Scott. 2012. Personal communication.

IMB Global Research, 2013. Personal communication.

Corbett, Steve and Brian Fikkert. 2009. *When Helping Hurts: How to Alleviate Poverty without Hurting the Poor.* Moody Publishers, Chicago, IL, USA.

Chapter 3
Understanding Poverty: A Key Before We Begin

Do you remember the nursery rhyme about the cat that went to London to visit the queen? She went to the royal palace and gained access into the royal chamber. All the ladies and gentlemen of the royal court were decked out in their finest attire. There was all the magnificence and pomp of the throne room with banners and golden decorations. There was even the presence of royalty herself dressed in the riches of the Kingdom.

However, when the narrator of the children's story asked the cat, "What did you see there?" The cat simply replied, "I saw a mouse under her chair." The simple lesson is that a cat sees a mouse anywhere because that is the nature of a cat.

All of us are blessed as well as cursed by the cultures to which we belong. Our individual and collective cultural biases give us a means for interpreting, living, and surviving in this world. My culture is deeply ingrained in the western, affluent culture of the United States. My personal bias has also been deeply influenced by many years spent in Asia working in development with the poorest of the poor. Nevertheless, I am who I am and even though I have many life changing experiences that have shaped my worldview, I, at the core, still see things from an affluent western perspective.

Who we are and how we view poverty deeply affects how we tend to address the problems and issues associated with poverty. How we view poverty is largely a product of how we have learned to view poverty. In other words, what we have been taught (consciously or subconsciously) about poverty shapes the way we view the poor and consequently our response (or lack thereof) to human suffering, oppression, and destitution.

For instance, those who have known nothing but poverty all their lives will surely have one view that is very different from my own since I have experienced a rather easy life. Moreover, those growing up in an Asian context will see poverty through a different set of lenses than myself who grew up in the southern United States. As an example, while growing up, I was always taught that if you really tried hard by getting your hair cut, getting cleaned up, and getting a job, you really did not have to be poor. In the world, this is not necessarily true.

Our experiences in life working together with our cultural biases also help to shape our view of poverty. Those of us privileged with the opportunity for years of education learn many things (right and wrong) about poverty as we climb the scholastic levels. Our religious experiences (or lack of) can be central in shaping our view as well as our actions towards poverty in the world. Our physical and emotional experiences of having face-to-face encounters with poverty shape us as well.

My Personal Early Life Experience

Growing up in rural Tennessee and being from a deeply religious family, I was privileged to have parents who were able to provide well for my physical, emotional, spiritual, and intellectual needs. I of course did not know at the time how privileged I was (especially compared to the rest of the world). My parents and the local country church that I grew up in tried to help me understand this by having a heart for helping the poor of our community.

I remember one Christmas holiday when I was about 10 years old. As a ministry project, every year our church put together baskets of food and delivered them to people in our community who were considered the "less fortunate." I really enjoyed doing this because I was taught (and truly felt) that this was a way of helping people and giving back a part of the blessings that we had received throughout the year.

We took the food baskets to pre-selected homes and gave them to the families. Sometimes we sang Christmas carols. Sometimes we prayed for the family. Many times, we just delivered the food baskets with a hearty, "God bless you. Merry Christmas!"

On one visit, an event occurred that was confusing to me for a number of years. We stopped at a particularly small, rundown house. We knocked on the door and the mother of the house greeted us. She seemed very happy to receive the food items and even as a young boy I could tell that the family did not have much. However, standing in the shadow of his mother, I noticed a young boy about my age and then realized that this was one of my classmates from the little rural school we attended.

When classes resumed the following month after the holidays, I noticed that this classmate who had been friendly before was now very standoffish and avoided me whenever he could. It was not until a few years later that he was able to share with me the reason. He was ashamed that we had come to his house and brought the food basket. He appreciated the food, but he literally hated me for a while because our church group had chosen his home to give a gift of food. From our perspective, they were poor. By anybody's measuring stick, they were needy. But the pain he experienced was that we judged them so even though we had good intentions.

Many years later when my wife and I started our development work in Asia, our mentor and friend in the work shared with us one of his truisms about helping the poor. He would often say, "The hardest thing to do is to really help a person." At first, I did not understand what this meant but over the years, I began to see the wisdom of this statement. In looking back to that boyhood experience with my less fortunate classmate, I really thought we were helping. I also thought that the way we helped was a good way. However, I have begun to see that it is very difficult to truly help people in a way that honors and builds them up but not create dependency or even resentment.

Misconceptions and Misperceptions

Jesus says in the gospel of Matthew, "You always have the poor with you, but you do not always have Me." (Matthew 26:11) As a young person, I was under the impression that this verse gave Christians a license for not having to care for the poor. Possibly this was from some overzealous revival speaker who used the passage as a proof text to warn us good Baptists of the evils of the social gospel. However misguided, this is not at all what the verse is saying. In fact, the verse has in actuality very little to do with the poor and much more to do with our devotion to Jesus.

It is interesting to note that this verse and accompanying story of Jesus' anointing for His burial is found in the three gospels of Matthew, Mark, and John but not in Luke. This is a rare occurrence in that Matthew, Mark, and Luke are generally called the "synoptic" or "see alike" gospels while John's is more unique. Moreover, except for a small addition in Mark's account, the statement made by Jesus in all three accounts is practically identical. The three quote Jesus as saying, "The poor you will always have with you, but you will not always have me." However, Mark inserts in the middle of that statement "and you can do what is good for them whenever you want," referring to "the poor." (Mark 14:7)

Maybe it was the statement "and you can do what is good for them whenever you want" which was preached from the pulpit (incidentally not by my pastor/mentor of many years) that was given as an excuse to not care for the poor. I distinctly remember hearing on more than one occasion, "See? Even Jesus said the poor would always be around, so therefore we should concentrate on evangelism."

I agree wholeheartedly that evangelism and disciple-making is the primary focus of the followers of Christ. However, I can find no evidence anywhere in the Bible that this relieves us of our social obligations such as caring for the poor and needy. As I have stated, I do not believe this verse is even addressing poverty.

The story is that Jesus is approaching the final hour and the cross. He is on the way to Jerusalem to die. Along the way He is teaching His disciples and followers truths that they will need to sustain them in the tumultuous days to come of his death, burial, and resurrection.

As Jesus visited the home of Simon the Leper, a woman named Mary (the sister of Lazarus who was raised from the dead) comes and anoints Jesus with an expensive perfume called "nard." When the disciples saw this, they criticized the woman for wasting a highly priced perfume. In John's account, he says that Judas Iscariot, the one who was later to betray Jesus, was the one who objected on the grounds that the perfume could have been sold and the money given to the poor. However, John goes on to tell us that Judas said this not because of his concern for the poor but rather because Judas was a thief and wanted to help himself to a cut of the profits.

But no matter the details of the anointing and the objections raised by the disciples, Jesus said to all present, "Leave her alone. Why are you bothering her? She has done a noble thing for Me. You always have the poor with you, and you can do what is good for them whenever you want, but you do not always have Me. She has done what she could; she has anointed My body in advance for burial. I assure you: Wherever the gospel is proclaimed in the whole world, what this woman has done will also be told in memory of her." (Mark 14:6-9)

What Jesus was saying in these passages was not to disassociate ourselves for concern of the poor but rather to focus on Him in all we say and do. There is nothing - evangelism, care for the poor, ministry - absolutely nothing that compares with the honor and privilege of knowing God and beholding Him.

Jesus was saying in His last moments before the cross, "Focus on me! I have a few short days to pour my last words of wisdom into you. We are in the last two minutes of the game. Focus!" It is not that we should neglect the poor but rather that we should focus on Jesus. It is the mirror of the story of Mary and Martha when Martha was busy making preparations for food and cleaning the house and complained to Jesus about Mary who was content with sitting at the feet of Jesus. Exasperated, Martha said, "Lord, don't you care that my sister has left me to do the work by myself? Tell her to help me!" Jesus replied, "Martha, Martha. You are worried and upset about many things, but only one thing is needed. Mary has chosen what is better, and it will not be taken away from her." (Luke 10:38-42)

Jesus could have just as easily said that we would always have the lost with us as well. Just the same, that would not give us a license to ignore the spiritual needs of those around us. In truth, by focusing on

Jesus and spending time with Him, it will make us even more committed to reaching out to the poor and downtrodden of the world.

How Do We See Poverty?

In Bryant Myers' book, *Walking with the Poor*, he gives an excellent account and detailed discussion of our views of the poor and how it affects not only the way we see the poor but also how we respond to them. He begins his chapter on poverty and the poor by warning us about the labels we use to describe the poor. As an example, if we were to make a list of all the words that would describe the poor, what would that list look like? More than likely, it would be composed of mainly negative terms and at the best neutral ones. For instance, in the first few pages of this chapter alone, I have used the terms "poor," "destitute," and "less fortunate."

According to Myers, many early development workers and theories centered on the assumption that poverty is basically a deficit of things. People lacked access and ownership to "things" that could make their lives better such as food, water, shelter, clothing, etc. Therefore, consequently, if we could find ways to provide "things" to poor people, we could help them out of their poverty. However, this leads to what Frances O'Gorman terms as the "band-aid" approach to helping the poor and leads to all sorts of problems of which dependency tops the list. Moreover, this approach is detrimental to the aid workers who are prone to develop a savior mentality in which they begin to see themselves as the salvation of the poor, thus reinforcing the dependency problems.

Another deficit often addressed by development workers is the deficit of skills and education of the poor. People can be classified as poor because they do not have the skills and knowledge to solve their problems associated with poverty. Therefore, if we can just give them more knowledge, better skills, and higher education, they will be able to come out of their poverty. As Myers says, this assumes that "if the poor simply learn enough, they will no longer be poor." This too, of course, is a flawed but surprisingly common view about poverty.

A third deficit seen by development workers according to Myers can come from the good intentions of religious development workers and organizations. For instance, Christian development workers/organizations might see poverty as a lack of the poor in their knowledge of God expressed in their ignorance of the good news of Jesus. This leads at times to a tendency of "doing development" for the sake of "getting to the people" with the gospel of Christ. This view and approach can lead to all sorts of misunderstandings as well as physically dangerous situations for field workers.

Again, citing Myers, if we view poverty as a deficit, this can lead to two great errors. One is that it stereotypes the poor and demeans them. Although not intentioned, our projections of this view on the poor can force them to begin to see themselves as we see them: inadequate, non-whole, and defective. As Myers says, this reinforces their view of themselves as marred in some way. This marred image then becomes a large factor that keeps them trapped in poverty.

The second great error is the attitude that we begin to form about ourselves as the savior of the poor. The role we play can skew our realities as to who we are and the effect that we can make on poverty. In short, we begin to believe (maybe subconsciously) that we are the ones who can save the poor. This attitude increases their poverty and tempts us to play god in the lives of the poor.

The Old Testament Concept of Poverty

As you read the Old Testament with an eye for God's concern for the poor, you cannot help but see the special place that He holds for the oppressed and afflicted of the world. Not many pages will go by before you deal with some story, some law, or some words of wisdom about the poor and their plight. Many of these words are directed at the rich and well off and come in the way of severe warnings how they should treat their less fortunate brothers and sisters.

Not only is God's concern for the poor evident, but also a pattern begins to emerge in which we can see that there are different types, or levels, of poverty that can come upon God's people. In several cases, poverty is due to poor choices such as laziness, chasing "fantasies," or even "haste" (see the book of Proverbs). Sometimes, poverty is voluntary, such as the bond slave who chooses to remain under the watchcare of his master by having his ear pierced with an awl at the doorpost of the house (Exodus 21:5-6). This is a "gentle" form of self-received poverty and is also a beautiful picture of how we can choose ourselves to be bound to God.

However, the most common form of poverty in the Old Testament is the non-voluntary type usually inflicted on the people through natural disasters, social upheavals, oppression, and wars. When we look at the history of Israel in the Old Testament we see basically five levels of poverty emerge. Bear in mind that you may not agree with all of these and may even be confused by the last one, but I am only describing what I see as illustrated in God's word. In later chapters, I will use some of these observations to make application to our present lives and the way we work with the poor.

Levels of Poverty in Old Testament Israel

1. A Loss of Things – The most basic level of poverty for Israel was a loss of their possessions. This occurred a number of times in their history and for differing reasons. Possessions and wealth were lost due to natural disasters. During one particularly long drought, Jacob (Israel) said to his sons, "Why do you keep looking at each other?...I have heard there is grain in Egypt. Go down there and buy some for us so that we will live and not die." (Genesis 42:1-2)

Possessions and wealth were frequently lost due to armed conflicts. Yet to be then King David, upon returning from an assembly with the Philistine Kings, returns with his men to his home base in Ziklag only to find that everything they owned and cherished (including their families) had been attacked and looted by the Amalekites. When they saw this, David and his men "wept loudly until they had no strength left to weep." (1 Samuel 30:4) In fact, the men were so distressed over their losses that they talked of stoning David to death (1 Samuel 30:6).

Possessions and wealth were also lost to oppression of some evil or ungodly ruler or power. At times, it was a foreign ruler or power that oppressed the Israelites and impoverished them. At other times, it was their own kings and leaders who mistreated the people. This brings us to the second level of poverty.

2. A Loss of Influence – When a person became poor in the Old Testament, a loss of possessions, if not quickly rectified, led to a loss of influence. The rich, as is often the case today, were the powerbrokers. They were the ones who had the influence to change things. Who would listen to the poor man? Who was the poor man to think that he would have a voice in any matter? In other words, being voiceless was the next level that people fell into when poverty became their constant companion.

In the story of the enslavement of the Jewish nation in Egypt, the people started out in a good relationship with the Egyptians and Pharaoh. Joseph, one of Jacob's sons, helped establish the Hebrews in a fairly rich area (Goshen) where they could survive and thrive during the drought years. However, Joseph died, generations came and went, and the Egyptian leaders forgot Joseph. They also became afraid of the Israelites who were growing numerous in their land. Therefore, a period of hundreds of years began in which the Israelites were enslaved into forced labor to build cities for the Egyptian leaders. The Bible says that the Egyptians "made their lives bitter with difficult labor in brick and mortar and in all kinds of fieldwork. They ruthlessly imposed all this work on them." (Exodus 1:14)

So why did the Israelites take the mistreatment? Why did they not just pack up and return to the Promised Land? After all, this mistreatment was building for 400 years. How could they fall so far from favor from the time of Joseph who rose to be only second to the King of Egypt in terms of power and authority? Since they were so numerous and powerful, why did they not just revolt and take over the country for themselves?

With the loss of Joseph there was a subtle change in their relationship to those who held power. The Israelites had lost their influence and the voice with access to the ear of those in power. At first, it was probably a minor change but nevertheless one with far reaching consequences. Undoubtedly, it was a part of God's overall plan for the forming of Israel as a nation. But the fact remains that Israel had lost its influence and voice among the Egyptians and slid into a different level of impoverishment.

In order to get their influence back and have a voice again in their future, God raised up a champion like no other (except for Jesus!) to be the voice of the Israelites and to restore the influence of His people. This pattern can be seen in other stories throughout the Old Testament as well.

God used a foreign king's cupbearer named Nehemiah to begin a great rebuilding of the city of Jerusalem. For over 100 years, God's choice city had lain in ruins. Israel had spent 70 years of exile in Babylon because of their unfaithfulness to God. They had lost everything. God then raised up a voice of influence, Nehemiah, who had the ear of the king.

God used a young Jewess named Hadassah, also known as Esther. Esther became the queen to King Xerxes, ruler over 127 provinces from India to Cush. When a plot emerged by an evil man named Haman to destroy all the Jews in the kingdom, God raised up Esther and her voice of influence with her husband, the king, to stop the plan and even reverse the anticipated outcome.

In each of these above cases, the people had not only lost their possessions but had also lost their influence and thus voice in any matter of their future development. And in most of these cases, God raised up a voice, usually in the form of a champion for God, who boldly voiced God's word.

3. A Loss of Identity – We also see in the Old Testament that when the people lose their possessions and their influence, they begin to lose their self-worth and in the most negative sense, their very selves. They become like ten of the twelve spies who were sent by Moses to spy out the Promised Land of Canaan and came back to the Israelites to report, "To ourselves we seemed like grasshoppers, and we must have seemed the same to them." (Numbers 13:33)

Those who arrive at this level of poverty become like the Israelites in the time of Gideon who, "Because of Midian, the Israelites made hiding places for themselves in the mountains, caves, and strongholds." (Judges 6:2) In other words, due to oppression, the Israelites literally had to take to the ground. They were the nation of God living underground in fear of the enemy. Time after time, God had worked a miraculous deliverance for them and they were the chosen people of God, but it is easy to forget who you are when poverty and oppression are at the door!

4. A Loss of Hope – In the view of Hebrew poverty, the slide of losses continues to the point where the people themselves experiencing the poverty begin losing any hope of deliverance. At this stage, the loss of possessions, influence, and identity are compounded to the point of confusion and despair. Social systems break down where hunger and problems are so severe that detestable practices such as cannibalism occur (2 Kings 6:24ff). A loss of hope also distorts reality where blame for the problems and corresponding solutions are sought out in areas apart from faith in and knowledge of God's prescribed ways.

One time, when famine was so severe in Samaria due to the attack of Ben-Hadad, king of Aram, the king of Israel decided to kill Elisha the prophet as a solution to his problem. The king states, "May God punish me and do so severely if the head of Elisha son of Shaphat remains on his shoulders today." (2 Kings 6:31) Praise be to God that Elisha stood in his faith and boldly pointed Israel back to the source of the problem (their sin) and the solution (utter trust and faith in God).

King Hezekiah cries out in the midst of his life-threatening illness, "Those who go down to the pit cannot hope for your faithfulness" (Isaiah 38:18). Job, when he had lost everything (possessions, influence, and identity) cries out, "What strength do I have that I should still hope? Is my strength that of stone, or my flesh made of bronze? Since I cannot help myself, the hope for success has been banished from me" (Job 6:11-13). The poor, at their deepest need, cry out, "Where will my help come from?" (Psalm 121:1)

This brings us to our fifth and final level of poverty as seen in the Old Testament. You may disagree with my observations and may even be shocked by them, but I think there is much evidence in the Bible to support the following final level of poverty. In a way, you might even call this the biblical definition of absolute poverty.

5. A Total Dependency on God – It almost seems strange to say that total trust in God is the final level of poverty. However, as we shall see, over and over the people of God had to come to the end of themselves to see the total sufficiency of God. In the end, when there was nowhere else to turn, when there were no armies, weapons, or resources of the people to save the day, when there was absolutely and positively no hope, there was God!

Ironically, many times in our abundance we fail to see God. And God wants wholeness, wellness, and justice for His people. But more often than not in Israel's case (as well as my own personal experience), it took some type of a calamity or destitution to make the people look back to God as their all in all sufficiency.

When God called Moses to go back to Egypt to lead in the deliverance of His people from captivity and slavery, He said, "I have observed the misery of My people in Egypt, and have heard them crying out because of their oppressors, and I know about their sufferings. I have come down to rescue them from the power of the Egyptians." (Exodus 3:7-8) When Pharaoh sent a massive army out to pursue and punish the Israelites, God showed He could be depended upon. Pharaoh had Israel hemmed up with their backs against the Red Sea with nowhere to go. As the Egyptian chariots came close, the Israelites "were terrified and cried out to the Lord." And God delivered them.

When the people occupied the Promised Land and were oppressed by other nations, the Bible says, "The Israelites cried out to the Lord" and he raised up a deliverer (Judges 3:9). In the story of Gideon, when the people cried out to the Lord because of the affliction upon them by the Midianites, God sent a prophet to remind them of His provisions, care for them, and to urge them to repentance (Judges 6:7-10).

The leaders of the Israelites, such as Moses and Joshua, constantly reminded the people of God's provisions for them when they cried out to Him for help (Numbers 20:16, Joshua 24:7). The prophets of Israel cried out to the Lord on behalf of the people, especially in times of distress (1 Samuel 7:9). Even the kings of Israel and Judah, often after they had exhausted other resources, cried out to the Lord with no hope of deliverance outside of divine intervention. This is best seen in the actions of Asa, the third king of Judah, when the Cushites marched out against him. The Bible tells us, "Then Asa cried out to the LORD his God: 'LORD, there is no one besides You to help the mighty and those without strength. Help us, LORD our God, for we depend on You, and in Your name we have come against this large army. Yahweh, You are our God. Do not let a mere mortal hinder You'" (2 Chronicles 14:11).

This absolute poverty as characterized by complete and total trust in God is nowhere better seen than in the Psalms of King David. As a man after God's own heart he writes, "I cry aloud to the LORD; I plead aloud to the LORD for mercy. I pour out my complaint before Him; I reveal my trouble to Him. Although my spirit is weak within me, You know my way. Along this path I travel they have hidden a trap for me… Listen to my cry, for I am very weak. Rescue me from those who pursue me, for they are too strong for me." (Psalm 142:1-6)

Therefore, an Old Testament definition of absolute poverty can be manifested as a total and complete trust in God. When all else fails, God prevails. When the arm and might falter, God will fight for us. When all the resources are consumed, God becomes our portion. And when there is no hope of deliverance, there is God!

Hebrew Concept of Charity

On the reverse side, when we look at views of charity in Hebrew thought, we find a mirror reflection of the views of poverty. In Robert

Lupton's book, *Compassion, Justice and the Christian Life*, he discusses the dangers of welfare and well-intentioned programs to help those in need, which oftentimes, in reality, handicap the people they were meant to help. He cautions, "Doing for others what they can do for themselves is charity at its worst…We must come to deeply believe that every person, no matter how destitute or broken, has something of worth to bring to the table."

He goes on to state that, "Welfare depletes self-esteem while honorable work produces dignity," citing four levels of true charity according to Hebrew thought. These are ways that we are to help the poor and needy and rank from the highest to the lowest in terms of providing help that truly helps and doesn't hinder.

The four levels of charity are:

1. Provide a job without the person's knowledge that you provided it
2. Provide a job where the needy knows you provided it
3. Give an anonymous gift to meet an immediate need
4. Give a poor person a gift with his full knowledge that you are the donor

The basic idea is that the best way to help a person in need is to give them a way, without them knowing who provided it, for them to work their way out of their problem. It is based on the principle that, "welfare depletes self-esteem while honorable work produces dignity."

Lupton goes on to talk about the difference between betterment and development. We are obviously working as a goal towards the latter: development. He states:

"Betterment does for others; development enables others to do for themselves. Betterment improves conditions; development strengthens capacity. Betterment gives a man a fish; development teaches him how and where to fish."

The New Testament View of Poverty

There are basically two Greek words in the New Testament that refer to poverty. There are derivations and different applications, but these two words in the noun form summarize what poverty is.

Penes refers to the poverty of a daily laborer or one who has to work for their daily bread. They are not among the absolute poor or destitute but are walking day to day in the reality of being needy. This word is used many times in connection with the word "needy" such as when the Bible refers to "the poor and needy."

Ptocheia is the Greek word for poverty that is even deeper and more severe than *penes* poverty. *Ptocheia's* modern day equivalent would be what we describe as absolute poverty. It literally means destitution. In the verb and adjective form, it often refers to the action of begging. While the *penes* poor are looked on in favor by God, it is the *ptocheia* poor who constantly seem to be the victims of injustices committed against them and thus have a special place in the sphere of God's care.

To be *ptocheia* poor is to be as poor as a beggar and, in reality, pretty much dependent on the mercy of others. Interestingly, it is also the word used by the Apostle Paul that describes Jesus Christ in 2 Corinthians 8:9, "for your sakes, he became poor." Jesus, according to Paul, chose voluntarily to experience *ptocheia* or "beggar" poverty on our behalf. This word is also used as a description of the church in Smyrna (Revelation 2:9) who, in the midst of *ptocheia* poverty and affliction is called rich because of their faith.

Selected Passages Dealing with Poverty

The topic of poverty is scattered all throughout the Bible. Yet there are some particular passages that stand out and give us some unique insights to the subject. Though not comprehensive, I will attempt to discuss a few of these selected passages in the following pages.

Deuteronomy 15:1-11 – No Poor Among You

In this passage, God institutes a system for taking care of poverty in the nation of Israel. "There will be no poor among you, however, because the LORD is certain to bless you in the land the LORD your God is giving you to possess as an inheritance if only you obey the LORD your God and are careful to follow every one of these commands I am giving you today." (Deuteronomy 15:4-5) What I hear

God saying in these verses is that in a world where God's laws are followed perfectly, there will be no poverty. Understanding that people and the inherent nature of sin make this world imperfect, God goes on in the same passage and exhorts the people to remember that, "There will always be poor people in the land. Therefore I command you to be openhanded toward your brothers and toward the poor and needy in your land." God says that the way we love and follow Him, manifested in the way that we deal with and treat our neighbors, has much to do with poverty and wealth.

Isaiah 58:1-9 – True Fasting

God, through the prophet Isaiah, is calling His people to repentance. He wants to restore His glory to fallen Zion. The nation is still intact, but it is wavering and stumbling like a punch-drunk prizefighter who has taken one too many blows. In this chapter, the prophet lets the nation of Israel know why they are falling, and much of it has to do with their treatment of the poor and needy.

The people seek after God's ways day to day. They seem eager to know His ways. They cry to the Lord, "Why have we fasted, but You have not seen? We have denied ourselves, but You haven't noticed!" (Isaiah 58:3)

The Lord replies, "Look, you do as you please on the day of your fast, and oppress all your workers,…You cannot fast as you do today, hoping to make your voice heard on high.…Isn't the fast I choose:

To break the chains of wickedness, to untie the ropes of the yoke, to set the oppressed free, and to tear off every yoke? Is it not to share your bread with the hungry, to bring the poor and homeless into your house, to clothe the naked when you see him, and not to ignore your own flesh and blood?" (Isaiah 58:3-7)

Then God tells Israel that if they repent, follow God and act justly towards their brothers, "Then your light will appear like the dawn, and your recovery will come quickly. Your righteousness will go before you, and the LORD's glory will be your rear guard. At that time, when you call, the LORD will answer; when you cry out, He will say, 'Here I am.' " (Isaiah 58:8-9) And he sums it up by saying, "If you get rid of the yoke among you, the finger-pointing and malicious speaking, and if you offer yourself to the hungry, and satisfy the afflicted one, then your light will shine in the darkness, and your night will be like noonday." (Isaiah 58:9-10)

I cannot find a more convincing passage in the entire Bible as to how our actions to our fellow man (and woman) can so affect our relationship with God. I also cannot find a more direct promise of the blessings that will occur when we spend our lives in the service of the poor.

Amos 5:11-15 – A Prophet's Wake Up Call

In his lament on the state of the nation of Israel, the prophet Amos writes a warning that those who have turned "justice into wormwood throw righteousness to the ground." (Amos 5:7) He decries Israel by saying, "you trample on the poor and exact a grain tax from him, you will never live in the houses of cut stone you have built; you will never drink the wine from the lush vineyards you have planted. For I know your crimes are many and your sins innumerable. They oppress the righteous, take a bribe, and deprive the poor of justice at the gates." (Amos 5:11-12) As a result, the prophet says that they, the people of Israel, have built mansions but will not live in them and they have planted lush vineyards but will not enjoy the fruit of their labor.

He then exhorts the people by saying, "Seek good and not evil so that you may live...Hate evil and love good; establish justice in the gate." Then, "Perhaps the LORD, the God of Hosts, will be gracious to the remnant of Joseph." (Amos 5:14-15)

Matthew 25:31-46 – About Sheep and Goats

Possibly, this is the most often quoted New Testament passage about caring for the poor and needy. Ironically, while referring to these things, it is probably a passage more concerned with the coming of Christ at the end of the ages.

Matthew gives us the picture of the triumphant Christ returning in all His glory, sitting on His throne and surrounded by His angels. All the nations are gathered before Him and "he will separate the people one from another as a shepherd separates the sheep from the goats." (Matthew 25:32-33) He places the sheep on His right (the favored group) and the goats on His left (the bad guys).

The separation is based upon our actions towards those who are poor and needy. How we have treated the hungry, thirsty, strangers, naked, sick, and prisoners seems to be the sole criteria for whether we will join the sheep (the blessed) or the goats (the cursed). Many will be confused because Jesus said, "For I was hungry and you gave me something to eat, I was thirsty…" and so on. The confused will say, "Lord, when did we see you hungry and feed you, or thirsty and give you something to drink?" Both the righteous and the unrighteous are confused in this story because they do not remember seeing Jesus in any of these conditions.

But Jesus replies to them, "I assure you: Whatever you did for one of the least of these brothers of Mine, you did for Me." (Matthew 25:40, 45) Then the righteous or those who treated the poor and needy with dignity will be invited to come as blessed of the Father. They are invited to come and take their inheritance that was prepared for them since the creation of the world. But woe unto the ones who have shown contempt for the poor and needy! "And they will go away into eternal punishment." (Matthew 25:46) Whatever your or my interpretation of this story is, it should serve as a stark warning about our obligation to minister to the poor and those in need.

James 2:1-13 – No Favoritism (contrast Leviticus 19:15)

At first, a cursory reading of this passage might be interpreted as extolling the virtues of poverty or, as I like to call it, an "Ode to Poverty." However, I find no evidence of the glorification of poverty or the romanticizing of it either in this passage or any other in the Bible. I do find a deep warning to the rich, however, as to how they treat the poor.

James uses this passage to give an ultimatum to those who would show favoritism to the rich over the poor. He warns them not to discriminate among themselves and in essence become "judges with evil thoughts." (James 2:4) He commands equitable treatment of the poor along with the rich. He even goes further by saying, "Listen, my dear brothers: Didn't God choose the poor in this world to be rich in faith and heirs of the kingdom that He has promised to those who love Him?" (James 2:5) To me, this hauntingly echoes the Sermon on the Mount where Jesus says, "You who are poor are blessed, because the Kingdom of God is yours." (Luke 6:20)

Again I have to balance this with saying that there is less to be said about poverty in this passage and more to be said about fair treatment of the poor. By contrast, the book of Leviticus gives us a similar warning with a slightly different twist. "You must not act unjustly when deciding a case. Do not be partial to the poor or give preference to the rich; judge your neighbor fairly." (Leviticus 19:15) Peter perhaps says it best in the book of Acts when he confesses to the family of Cornelius, "Now I really understand that God doesn't show favoritism, but in every nation the person who fears Him and does righteousness is acceptable to Him." (Acts 10:34-35) However James does clearly warn us that there are special woes awaiting the people who show favoritism for the rich and also oppress the poor. God's message is simply this: do not mess with the helpless unless you want to face the consequences!

2 Corinthians 8:8-9 – The Poverty of Christ

In his encouragement of the Corinthian believers to be generous in their giving, the apostle Paul gives a beautiful picture of how Christ voluntarily took poverty upon Himself to save us and bring us into the richness of His kingdom. He says, "For you know the grace of our Lord Jesus Christ: Though He was rich, for your sake He became poor, so that by His poverty you might become rich." (2 Corinthians 8:9)

Just imagine! The Lord of the entire universe, the second person of the triune God, the Beloved Son, became flesh and dwelt among us. He left the glory, splendor, and majesty of heaven to come to earth in the form of a baby, born to commoners, Mary and Joseph. He was born not into wealth that His exalted position deserved but in a stable because there was no room for Him at the local inn. He grew up in the home of a carpenter and made friends with mostly fishermen and tradesmen as He began His ministry. He chose obedience even to death on a cross, a punishment reserved for common criminals. He did all this and more in order that we, through faith in who He is and what He did, might have abundant life. Amazing! Never has anyone given up so much for so many.

A View of Poverty in the Gospel of Luke

I would like to conclude this biblical view of poverty by looking at what the gospel of Luke has to say about the topic. All the other gospels have many of the same verses as well as other references to the poor, but Luke seems to have a special place in his heart for the poor. Maybe it comes from his medical background and his heart for alleviating physical suffering. Perhaps it is for some other reason; I do not know. However, Luke does give a special account of and consideration to the poor of the world.

Luke begins his focus on the poor by telling us an account of Jesus who inaugurates His ministry by proclaiming, "The Spirit of the Lord is on Me, because He has anointed Me to preach good news to the poor. He has sent Me to proclaim freedom to the captives and recovery of sight to the blind, to set free the oppressed, to preach the acceptable year of the Lord." (Luke 4:18-19) This announcement comes at the beginning of Jesus' ministry and occurs at the synagogue on the Sabbath in His hometown of Nazareth. Jesus is basically quoting from Isaiah 61:1-2, but He leaves no doubt that He is referring to Himself. The reaction of the local people confirms this. His announcement as Messiah as well as His heart for the poor is revealed.

Luke then includes the poor in his recounting of the Sermon on the Mount. Where Matthew records, "The poor in spirit are blessed" (Matthew 5:3), Luke simply records, "You who are poor are blessed, because the kingdom of God is yours." (Luke 6:20) I have read a lot of commentaries on this verse, of which many try to explain away who Jesus means as "the poor." Some even say that this is really the poor in Spirit as stated in Matthew's account. I beg to differ. I think it means exactly what it says. It is not a statement that extols the blessings of poverty but it does say something about the poor and their proximity to God and His Kingdom. We will talk about this more later.

Jesus does use the same occasion to sternly warn the rich. He says, "But woe to you who are rich, for you have received your comfort. Woe to you who are now full, for you will be hungry." (Luke 6:24-25)

The third account of Luke's addressing the poor comes at a time when Jesus uses His caring for the poor and helpless as proof of His being the Messiah as well as words of comfort for his cousin, John. John (the Baptist) is in prison. He is about to lose his life because of the obscene dance of a teenager. He is full of fear, doubt and in need of some reassurance. He sends some of his followers to Jesus to ask Him, "Are You the One who is to come, or should we look for someone else?" (Luke 7:20)

Interestingly enough, instead of replying simply with a yes or a no, Jesus said to the messengers, "Go and report to John the things you have seen and heard: The blind receive their sight, the lame walk, those with skin diseases are healed, the deaf hear, the dead are raised, and the poor are told the good news." (Luke 7:22) It is noteworthy that Jesus expected John to understand that only the Messiah, the one sent from God, could have that kind of concern and heart for the poor, downtrodden, and suffering.

On another occasion, Luke tells us that Jesus had opportunity to talk with the well-to-do Pharisees about their attitudes and treatment of the poor and needy. He had been invited to the home of a prominent Pharisee to eat a meal. After reclining at the table, the Pharisee noticed that Jesus did not wash before the meal and was surprised. Jesus used the moment to talk about inward cleansing as opposed to outward ritual, and he used treatment of the poor as the case study. Jesus said to them, "Now you Pharisees clean the outside of the cup and dish, but inside you are full of greed and evil. Fools! Didn't He who made the outside make the inside too? But give from what is within to the poor, and then everything is clean for you." (Luke 11:39-41)

In the same passage, Jesus goes on to warn them about their tithing. They gave a tenth of their mint, rue and other garden herbs but neglected justice and love of God. They were lovers of the best seats in the synagogues and thus the place of honor among men. Because of their attitudes, largely dealing with their heart towards those less fortunate, Jesus pronounced, "Woe to you! You are like unmarked graves; the people who walk over them don't know it" (Luke 11:44).

Not long after this, Jesus was teaching His disciples and urging them not to worry excessively over earthly needs. He said that life is more than food and the body is more than clothes. He cited the example of the ravens and the lilies: they do not sow or reap, they do not toil or spin and yet God cares for them. He tells them to seek the kingdom of God and let God provide for them.

He then says, "Don't be afraid, little flock, because your Father delights to give you the kingdom. Sell your possessions and give to the poor. Make money-bags for yourselves that won't grow old, an inexhaustible treasure in heaven, where no thief comes near and no moth destroys. For where your treasure is, there your heart will be also" (Luke 12:32-34).

This story is followed up shortly by the tale of a rich ruler. The young man came to Jesus and asked Him what he needed to do in order to inherit eternal life. Jesus told him to obey the laws of Moses. The young ruler replied that he had kept all the laws since he was a boy. To which Jesus replied, "You still lack one thing: Sell all that you have and distribute it to the poor, and you will have treasure in heaven. Then come, follow Me." Luke then tells us that the young man went away very sad because he was a man of great wealth (Luke 18:18-23).

In Luke 14, Jesus exhorts people that when they give a feast or banquet, they are not to invite their friends, relatives, or rich neighbors but rather the poor, crippled, lame, and blind. The reason is that they, unlike your rich acquaintances, cannot repay you. Instead, you will be repaid at the resurrection of the righteous for your acts (Luke 14:12-14).

This passage parallels the story of a tax collector named Zacchaeus. Zacchaeus was shown compassion by Jesus even though he was a scoundrel of a tax collector who had defrauded countless people out of their money. When Zacchaeus came face to face with Jesus, he repented of his sin and experienced the grace of God. This was evidenced and reported by Luke with Zacchaeus saying, "Look, I'll give half of my possessions to the poor, Lord! And if I have extorted anything from anyone, I'll pay back four times as much!" To this Jesus replied, "Today salvation has come to this house." (Luke 19:1-10)

Finally, Luke concludes his references and stories of poverty by telling of a widow who gave an offering to God even though she was very poor. Jesus saw the rich put their gifts into the temple treasuries in abundance. He also saw the poor widow who was only able to put in two small coins. "'I tell you the truth,' He said. 'This poor widow has put in more than all of them. For all these people have put in gifts out of their surplus, but she out of her poverty has put in all she had to live on'" (Luke 21:1-4).

Lessons I Have Learned from Working with the Poor

1. The poor are people. The truth is that they are people like us who are also created in the image of God. One of the greatest things that a development worker can learn to do is to view the poor from God's perspective and to also help them begin to see themselves in the same light. Remember ten of the twelve Israelites who went to spy out the Promised Land and later came back to say, "We even saw the Nephilim there--the descendants of Anak come from the Nephilim! To ourselves we seemed like grasshoppers, and we must have seemed the same to them." (Numbers 13:33) When we stop viewing the poor through our labels and acknowledge them as people, we take a huge step toward being able to work with them in a healthier way.

2. The poor have an amazing capacity for solving their own problems. This lesson could be thought of as an extension of the first one. When we get to the point of seeing the poor as people, we begin to realize the amazing capacity they have in solving their own problems if given a chance. They are not helpless in most cases. If we see them as helpless, we will often fall prey to the temptation to ride into their poverty on the white horse of technology or our own resources to "save them" from their plight. In doing so what we tend to accomplish is to further impoverish them through creation of unhealthy dependencies on us or our programs. As well, this robs them of the right to grow and learn how to address their chronic problems. If our strategies are filled with things we do for the poor, the results of our work will largely be window dressing and in the long run, more than likely be detrimental instead of beneficial to the poor with whom we work. I have seen this firsthand. I have also seen the amazing capacity of the poor, when given the right opportunities and catalytic input, to come together and not only solve problems but also develop capabilities to solve future problems. More importantly, I have seen the poor come together in community to be able to move ahead and even grow in their ability and skills to tackle increasingly complex issues affecting them.

3. The poor in general understand community better than I do as a community development worker. When our staff began making the transition from a project-driven organization to a community/needs-driven one, it was easy but errant to assume that we actually

knew what communities should look like and be like. In our innocent arrogance, we worked hard to come together as a staff of development workers and come up with the vision of the model community and village. As I look back on this, I think it was a great exercise and helped us to envision what we considered to be a fully developed community. However, in doing so, we mistakenly cast our projections of community on many of the villages with whom we began to work.

As we began to apply our community development techniques and programs to our extension sites, we quickly learned the valuable lesson that community is a very complex organism. To change one small part has great implications on the community as a whole. Moreover, the insiders of the community always had a deeper insight into their community and the particular reasons as to why they looked a certain way or did things in a different way than what we considered "correct." Taking time to work with communities by listening to them helped us to see the value of local knowledge and ways.

Not only did we find that the villagers tended to know more about their own particular community than we did as outsiders, but we also found that in many cases they knew more about community as a whole. For instance, in the initial stages of our work, one of the basic strategies included in our vision for the ideal community was that there would be functioning groups within the community. The groups would be responsible for the development moving forward during and even after the outsiders' participation with the group. This was how we viewed our development work as becoming sustainable.

In other words, there would be a core group or core groups developed in the community to make sure that our vision of fair and equitable development was taking place and continuing on past the time of our involvement and presence in the community.

We quickly learned that the community already had existing groups and understood to a large degree how community was supposed to function. We also learned that the insiders (the community) had a keen insight and more importantly a historical perspective on what it took for them to function as community. Dropping in at a particular point in time of the history of a community is probably the worst way to understand a community. So many things happen that are hidden or automatically understood by the community that it is hard for an outsider (like me) to see and appreciate. What I learned was that it was necessary to first of all learn from the community because they possess a wealth of knowledge about themselves.

4. I have a lot of fear and insecurities to overcome if I am to work with the poor. This was one of the hardest lessons for me to learn. Have you ever held a baby with fever and wondered if you were going to get sick? Has a village child ever sat in your lap and because of his condition, you felt like lice were now crawling on you? Many of our staff have dealt with these feelings and much more. One co-worker once shared with me that her greatest fear was that the poor with whom she worked were going to ask her for things such as money, food, etc. When we have fears and insecurities in dealing with the poor, it is easy

to withdraw and isolate ourselves in offices or the business of writing materials and not really engage people with the true love of Christ.

5. I have a lot of cultural constraints to overcome in order to work with the poor. Being from a relatively affluent society and family, I have a severe limitation in understanding poverty, the poor and in many instances, the decision process of communities in poverty. When I judge the insider problems from my outsider perspective, it is often very hard for me to see their line of thought and decision-making. Moreover, because of my problem-solving cultural bias, it is tempting for me to become the one to solve all of their problems with "obvious" solutions. It is not that I am unaware of the dangers of doing this. The thing I struggle with is that I do it so automatically (help solve people's problems for them without involving them in the process) that it is hard for me to stop myself from doing so.

6. I have to constantly examine my heart, motives and actions in working with the poor. I would like to think that all of my motives are noble and pure. However, I know my own heart too well to be fooled by this notion. Sometimes there are motives of recognition from others. At other times there are desires of approval from others for my humanitarian acts and the results that we obtain. At some points there are deep cultural and social values that drive me which may or may not be held by those with whom I am deeming to "help." I would strongly suggest that a person considering involvement in working with the

poor to not only initially but constantly evaluate their heart and goals as to their motives of desiring to do so.

7. God blesses and honors our efforts of working with the poor. It is not magic. It is not a secret recipe. However, I can give testimony to the fact that this is true: God does amazingly bless our efforts of working with the poor. I have seen it happen over and over. It is like yeast in dough or bread cast upon the water. Our tiny efforts, done in the name of Christ, spread to areas that we could never imagine. What I have found is that Christ proclaimed through word and deed is the most effective means of reaching people sustainably for His kingdom. I have found truth in the admonition to "preach the gospel" but have discovered equal value in "teaching them to obey all that I have commanded."

Chapter Summary

• There are many misconceptions and misperceptions of what poverty is and how we should address it. We need to understand poverty from both a biblical and cultural perspective.

• How we view and understand poverty largely determines how we address it.

• We can learn much from those with less resources than ourselves if we will only seek to understand first.

References

Myers, Bryant L. 1999. *Walking With the Poor: Principles and Practices of Transformational Development.* Orbis Books, Maryknoll, New York.

Lupton, Robert. 2007. *Compassion, Justice and the Christian Life: Rethinking Ministry to the Poor.* Regal Books, Ventura, CA, USA.

Chapter 4
Engaging the Community for the Kingdom

How do we enter a community with the purpose of Kingdom-focused community development? How do we even identify those areas that should be priorities for our work?

We need to consider a number of things as we begin to think about entering a new community/area of work with development as a goal.

- Who are we in relation to the community? What is our identity? Are we a development organization, or are we just concerned people? A clear understanding by the whole team and a unified identity is essential, especially in creative access areas.

- What and who is our target? Is it a certain people group or population segment? Is it small enough/large enough that if we are successful in our program that we will accomplish our overall goals? What are the security risks/hazards that would possibly derail our work?

- What is the appropriate level of entry? Do we need to begin at the top down such as working with high level government officials? Or do we need to go directly to a village and begin with a local person/council?

- What are our overall goals and objectives? How will we know when we reach those? What is the vision for what we want to accomplish?

Remember that the more we know ourselves, our target communities, and our goals and objectives, the more likely we are to accomplish our goals. Also remember that our posture should be that of learners all throughout the community development process. Most importantly, always keep in mind that we are doing this to affect both physical and spiritual development.

As we enter a community, we have these things in mind and we have the community development tools in hand. But as we initiate engagement, we do so with a focus on:

1. Trust building
2. Having clear and agreed upon expectations (with the participating community)
3. Constantly looking for the powerbrokers and decision makers in the group
4. Finding out the positive things as well as the problems that the community is experiencing
5. Acknowledging that the community was developing long before you or I got there and it will be developing long after we leave

Do Your Homework

If we see community development in a Kingdom framework as a strategy for missions, we should have some premises and goals beforehand. We should be looking for the areas and communities that are underdeveloped and in need of help. We should also be looking for strategic spiritual areas of need as well. One guiding principle that we have used is to look for the areas where great physical need overlaps with great spiritual need. We then would use these criteria to select target areas of our Kingdom-focused community development efforts.

The determinants of physical needs for a certain area/people can usually be gathered from government or Non-Government Organization (NGO) sources. Information such as poverty indices, infant mortality rates, literacy (especially in women), comparative incomes, etc., is readily available and serves as a good secondary source indicator of actual situations.

The determination of spiritual needs is sometimes a bit more challenging to gather. There are resources such as Operation World, the Joshua Project, etc., that can give us some initial indication of spiritual need. Criteria such as church to population ratio, access to the gospel (in various forms – written, oral, media, etc.), number of other groups targeting the people group/population segment being considered, etc., can help identify larger as well as smaller spiritually needy segments.

If we are working in the 10/40 Window or least-reached areas of the world, it may well be that any location or any people group with whom we choose to work will score high in both physical and spiritual needs. However, a little homework and research beforehand can sometimes help to steer us to areas of hidden need.

We used this approach in the southern Philippines. We had been working for years with poverty alleviation and church planting among rural tribal people groups. We had done much good work both in the physical as well as the spiritual development areas. But we wanted to look at our efforts and especially future ones in a new way. We chose to gather data and develop a physical index of need that we could overlay with a spiritual index of need. What we found changed the whole focus of our team's ministry. We found that there were huge areas of people groups that we were not engaging that scored high on both indexes and that the majority of our work was with high physical needs but relatively low spiritual needs. The simple discovery led to us reprioritizing our efforts to focus on the most underdeveloped and spiritually unreached.

Do Your Knee-work and Legwork

The initial research (homework) that we did turned out to be only the first step in a longer process. After identifying huge areas of overlooked needs, we desired to get some "boots on ground" to help verify what was accurate. We began by praying for God's wisdom to find the areas He would have us work. Everything equal, we determined that we could pretty much choose any area in the larger area/people groups that we began to target and we would definitely be in the midst of physical and spiritual poverty. However, we desired to find the best places – or more importantly – the divinely appointed places for us to begin our work.

Through prayer and much discussion together, we began to identify some key areas that we thought would be good initial entry points. In some of the areas we knew people and had relationships that might serve as facilitators of our community development workers into the community. Others seemed to be key areas such as crossroads/market towns for a larger area. We began to develop plans and timelines to send our people out – two by two – to see if we could find where God was leading us to work.

Look for the Person of Peace

One of the keys of entry into a community, from a biblical perspective, is to find the person of peace. As this is true in missions with regard to evangelism and church planting efforts, it is also true with community development.

After we have identified major potential entry areas/communities and begin on-ground exploration of the areas, we generally find a person or persons of peace or influence that facilitate our entry into that area/community. Sometimes this can come in the form of the obvious – a local government official or a power person in the community. At other times it can be a person of little influence such as a farmer or a grandmother who "gets it" in terms of development. The key is that as our development workers enter community, they are prayerfully and constantly on the outlook for that person.

We distinguish between the person of peace and the person of influence. In some cases, they are the one and the same. However, they can be different. The person of influence is the person who facilitates our entry into the community and gives us as outsiders an initial "acceptance" into the community. The person of peace is the person who facilitates the spiritual connection with the community and is usually open to the message of the gospel.

In one of our projects in the Philippines, we started targeting an unreached people group that we had previously overlooked. While we were praying and strategizing how and where to begin engaging the group, the Lord sent a handful of young men from that people group to our training center. They came with the purpose to learn about better agriculture and health care practices for their communities but within that group, some were also hungry for spiritual truths and learning about Jesus. They had seen Him in a dream and were told that they could learn about Him if they came to us. It is interesting to note that the timing of their dreams corresponded closely with our praying for wisdom and knowledge as to how to access their people group.

Over time, most of that original group served as persons of influence to allow us access to their communities and thus our new targeted areas. By following up on their agriculture and health care training, we were given influence and thus access to their home communities. However, only two or three of those served as persons of peace. These served not only to give access to their communities but became transformed persons themselves (through faith in Christ) and were avenues to their communities for not only physical but spiritual development as well.

Transition from Person of Peace to Community

While we may begin and gain entry into a community through one person or relationship, we want to move quickly towards interaction with the whole community or at least a significant segment. Ideally, we would allow the person of peace/influence to lead us to others. However, we need to be on guard against those who would monopolize our time and exclude us from community involvement.

John 4 Model: The Woman at the Well

In John chapter 4, we find a great example of a person of peace: the Samaritan woman at the well. After a long day of travelling, Jesus had come to rest by a well in the town of Sychar. His disciples had gone ahead to obtain needed supplies. A woman of Samaria came to draw water and Jesus asked her for a drink. The woman was taken aback because Jesus was Jewish and the Jews were known not to associate with Samaritans.

Through a series of questions and thought provoking dialogue, Jesus confronted the woman with God's truth and revealed Himself as the Messiah. As the disciples returned from their errands, the woman ran back to her community and proclaimed, "Come, see a man who told me everything I ever did! Could this be the Messiah?" The result was that "many Samaritans from that town believed in Him because of what the woman said." Jesus stayed on with them for a few days, teaching further the truths of God, and many more believed. They believed not only because of what the woman said, but because "we have heard for ourselves and know that this really is the Savior of the world."

While this is mostly a spiritual encounter with regard to a person of peace, it does highlight a number of key points worth noting:

1. A person of peace is usually hungry and looking for truth. The Samaritan woman was coming to the well to get water. But it is obvious that her heart was heavy. She seemed to be tired of life. She had run through her bevy of men. She had come to the same well hundreds of times. Surely there was more meaning to life than this.

2. A person of peace is open to new relationships and new ideas. The Samaritan woman knew all the standard answers and the history of her people, but she also knew that there were gaps in her understanding. Jesus filled in the gaps with the truth of the Scriptures and thus moved her towards hearing the ultimate truth of who He was.

3. A person of peace is willing to step out of his/her cultural norms. It was a bit of a stretch for a woman to engage in conversation

with a stranger, let alone a man.

4. A person of peace is willing to introduce others into their community and serve as a go-between. In this case, when she heard that Jesus was the Messiah, she immediately left her water jar, went into the town, and began to tell others about Jesus.

5. A person of peace usually becomes a servant of the Prince of Peace as well as a key component to the changes that happen and continue in the community.

Chapter Summary

• There are a number of things to consider as we begin to think about entering and engaging a new community.

• We need to do our homework, knee-work, and leg work as we prepare to engage communities.

• The biblical model of a person of peace is helpful for us as we enter into a new community.

Chapter 5
The Community Development Process

As stated earlier in Chapter 2, community development is a process communities enter in order to be able to become better at meeting their own needs. It focuses on people working together in interdependency to take charge of their situations and move toward a more empowered and satisfying life as individuals as well as for the good of the whole group. When we work in community development, the focus is on what the community does, not what our organization's goals are. It puts people first over projects, programs, production, and paperwork.

Community development is more about "how" people solve their problems and less about "what" they actually do. Simply stated, individuals and communities desire good projects such as new roads, schools, electricity, safe drinking water, etc. However, as community developers, we are focused more on "how" they arrive at these ends. Our goal is not simply the physical improvements that happen in a community but the social, emotional, and spiritual changes that occur as well.

A focus on the process of our development work and approaches helps us to keep an eye on sustainable development. Any individual or organization can fund projects and claim physical success given resources and time in a community. However, the way that these projects or programs are implemented has numerous immediate and future effects on the communities that are often missed by fly-by-night development workers and organizations.

Several years ago, I was asked to help evaluate a micro-enterprise project that had taken place in a particular country. By most every physical measurement, the project was a success. Within a three-village area, income had been documented to have doubled in approximately a two-year project time span. Through the introduction of a new "business," people statistically were more well off (almost 100% across the board) than they were before.

However, closer analysis of the program showed some deep flaws. Local people were asking, "If we have more money, then why do we not see an improvement in our lives?" When the "extra income" generated by the project was measured and qualified as to usage, a stark fact was realized. The survey of "extra income" spent showed that since the major decision makers and controllers of the projects were the men in the communities, almost all of the extra money generated went to their priorities (gambling, alcohol consumption, and tobacco).

In community development, attempts are made to invest in the whole community and to monitor and measure what is really happening in the lives of the community as projects and programs unfold. Moreover, the tools employed in the community development process help to raise the voice of the marginalized and get people working together for the good of the whole. A basic belief is that people working and growing together as community can do far more than individuals or narrowly focused groups.

Community Development as Kingdom Development

If community development is a process in which communities enter to be able to become better at meeting their own needs, "Kingdom development" is this along with an eternal focus. Kingdom development workers see at the very core of underdevelopment a spiritual problem: sin. Man (and woman) is in poverty, pain, and suffering. This is not only due to circumstances of environment, poor choices, or even oppression by others, but also because of the web of lies and evil that came with the fall of man in the Garden of Eden. Just as sin and death came into this world with one man, Adam, so did the offspring of poverty, injustice, and disenfranchisement.

Many physical, social, and emotional problems can be overcome by people working together in interdependency. This is a core strategy of community development. However, the Kingdom developer recognizes the most needed change as being the very heart of individuals and communities alike. In fact, this "heart change" is the very foundation serving as a precursor to true Kingdom development.

In Kingdom development, community, above all else, is about right and restored relationships. It is about right relationships between man and God. It is about rightly restored relationships of man to fellow man based upon man's correct relationship to the Creator God. And it is about right relationships of man to God's creation, the world.

Sin and death, through the choice of Adam, the first man, brought about chaos and a loss of Eden. Eden, more than symbolically, is seen as the original plan that God had for man and all his offspring. In the Bible we see this plan unfold in the full restoration of a new heaven and new earth and humankind fully restored in right relationship to God after all is said in done (Revelation 21 and 22).

Here then is the foundation of Kingdom development: the individual as well as the community restored to a right relationship with God through the blood of His only begotten Son, Jesus Christ. This relationship then becomes the springboard and even the wellspring of creating and restoring community relationships of man to man and man to God's creation. Kingdom development, like community development, is a process entered into by people in order to become what God meant them to be from the beginning of time. These are whole communities, experiencing life to the full (John 10:10b). These are individuals and communities alike who hear and obey the voice of the Good Shepherd. And these are people, under the Lordship of Jesus Christ, working together to solve their problems with interdependency on one another (the community) yet with total dependency on God!

Kingdom development and our efforts at addressing the deepest needs of people is a foreshadowing and even an attempt at what life is really meant to be and will be in an eternity spent with God the Father, the Son, and the Holy Spirit. Kingdom development on earth is our preparation for life eternal with the King and with the community of our fellow believers.

A New Paradigm of Measuring "Success"

In community development, we are looking from a whole new paradigm when measuring success of a project or program. The main focus is the community and what happens in the members and collective group. It is not our organizational goals or how well we do our work but rather how well the community comes together to solve their problem(s). It is also about what they have learned and what attitudes have been changed to allow them to address other problems. In addition, from a Kingdom development standpoint, we want to see individuals and communities move towards a lifestyle that is reflective of God's word and plan for people.

Figure 1. Examples of success measurements for development projects:

traditional versus Kingdom development

◇◇

Traditional Success Measurements

Number of projects completed

Program stayed within budget

Projects completed on time

Projects are good quality

All goals accomplished

Kingdom Success Measurements

Capabilities built within the community

Capacities of people enhanced

Better community is formed

Greater confidence for the future built

Community/People more Christ-like

Of course we rejoice when people are helped whether in their acute needs or chronic needs. We are happy to see people gain access to food and clean water. We are happy to see them get better roads and health care facilities for their villages. However, as Kingdom development workers, we are not just satisfied with the physical aspects. We are also consciously looking for development of the following in the people with whom we work:

1. Capabilities – These are abilities, skills, and knowledge that people need to solve their local problems. In cases of initial community development projects, local capabilities are sufficient to accomplish the task. We are constantly amazed at what local knowledge and abilities are available to the local community. They are often hidden or simply overlooked until the community members come together and begin to identify them themselves. In one village project where water was determined as the primary need (and eventually the initial project which the community tackled), after a series of resource mappings and

planning, the local group not only identified local materials they could use to construct the water system but also two local villagers who had the skills and knowledge to design and implement the project. However, in many cases, new skills and knowledge are needed to solve the community problems. This is especially true as they move into more and more complex problems.

2. Capacities – Capacities are different from capabilities in that they are abilities in which the community can go outside themselves to get help for a particular project. One of the greatest capacity expanders is when community members begin to learn and value the art of networking. Networking can and should be done with outside government officials and institutions, other non-Government organizations, private donors, etc. A growth in this area of a community means that they are able to address more and more complex problems and situations that are keeping them in an underdeveloped state.

3. Community – As the villagers/community members work together toward solving their problems, how well do they become "community"? How is their capacity for caring for and loving one another enhanced by our program? If they get good physical projects but in the process come to hate one another, is this success or failure? One of the reasons we focus on the "how" they get to a particular project is the fact we want to see community strengthened and built up. A development program that trades off short term quick results for good process and good relationships/interaction among people is one that is destined for problems. Remember, from a development workers' view,

the new paradigm focus is on what happens in the lives of the people rather than how many projects they implement or how many things that they check off their accomplishment list. I have personally seen some very good community development programs that did not show a lot of physical progress in the first couple of years. However, these programs were focused on building things like capacity, capabilities, and good community and in time, produced wonderful results.

4. Confidence – When the community comes together, when capabilities and capacities are expanded, and when success with small projects begins to happen, the community begins to gain a new confidence in the fact that they can do something to change their situation. From a poverty standpoint, this is a very critical thing to build because many poor communities have experienced failure to the point that they believe that they cannot change things and thus settle into an acceptance and even fatalistic mode. When people working together begin to have success – even small successes – it makes all the difference in their outlook and willingness to move on to other issues. Again, the measurement of success has more to do with what happens in people and communities rather than the actual projects they complete.

5. Christ-likeness/Character – The final measurement in the new paradigm of success is the Christ-likeness of the members of the community and the community as a whole. True Christ-likeness can only be expressed through a regenerated heart filled with the Holy Spirit. However, any move towards Christ-likeness by individuals and communities can be small steps towards making temporal and eternal dif-

ferences in the lives of the people with whom we work. We know that God blesses people and communities who walk according to His ways. In the Bible, not only did He bless His people (Israel and the Church) who followed Him but He also blessed the aliens and outsiders as well such as Naaman the leper (2 Kings 5) and Cornelius of Caesarea (Acts 10). These are but two examples where God blesses when He is honored and His ways are followed. Naaman was obedient to the word of God through the prophet Elisha and was healed of leprosy. Cornelius' prayers were answered by God because he and his family were God-fearing, prayed regularly, and gave generously to those in need. In our community development efforts, when we see Kingdom values beginning to become commonplace in the communities in which we work, we are beginning to see God's kingdom come. And this becomes fertile ground for His blessing to be poured out and a greater opportunity for His name to be made known.

A Simple Gauge of Whether Our Community Development has a Kingdom Impact

There are three words or concepts that we can ask regarding our community development efforts that help reveal whether or not we are engaging in Kingdom impactful development. I attribute this simple test to one of our workers in Asia who uses these as a gauge of true Kingdom development and impact.

1. Participatory – Are our efforts truly participatory, involving the local community in all aspects of the development process? In other words, whose development is it? Whose problems and whose solutions? Do the local people own the process from the very beginning through the implementation and evaluation of their projects? Participatory implies action on both the outsiders (development workers) and the insiders (community). The healthy trend should be a growing participation and involvement from the local community and a diminishing input from the outsiders.

2. Transformational – Is true transformation taking place in the community due to our efforts? Not only are improvements being made such as better roads, clean water, and more income, but are there also improvements in the spiritual climate of the community? Are more biblical values being embraced? Are more people hearing the truth about God? And most importantly, are more lives being transformed by God's Spirit? Transformation implies not just visible, measurable differences in the community but transformed hearts and lives.

3. Sustainable – Are our efforts to help the community sustainable? More importantly, is the process the community has experienced and the resulting improvements to their lives and community sustainable? Sustainability is basically the ability of a thing or system to be self-supporting and perpetual of and in its own self or resources. Is what the community accomplished and the new skills and capacities

gleaned going to go on once we leave or will they be abandoned? This is a good question both for the physical and spiritual changes incurred by the target community.

The Process Explained

The development process on which the development worker focuses includes basically five steps. We have revised the original process, combining some of the steps and reducing the number of steps from eight to five. The fewer number of steps help us to remember them better as well as make them easier to teach to others.

Regardless of the number of steps used, by focusing on good processes, the development worker helps to develop the people of the community. This leads to a number of benefits. It also leads to sustainability of the development work in that people not only gain "projects" but also other tangible benefits enabling them to expand their projects and tackle new and increasingly more complex problems faced by the community.

Even though the explanation that follows is linear and sequential, this process should be considered as circular and free flowing. Generally, a good community development program follows these steps (or similar ones). However, these are not concrete steps that can be followed as a recipe for guaranteed success.

Additionally, at best, the development worker is a catalyst and facilitator in the process, not the main actor. The community is the main actor. We understand from personal and organizational constraints that our time as outsiders in a community will be limited. That limited time is best spent focusing on the process described and not the project's physical results (e.g. roads, water systems, and better income).

As catalysts, we commonly spend anywhere from one to five years in a particular community. Three years is about the average time we need to accomplish our goal of getting people working and growing together as community. Again, this is not a hard and fast rule but rather an average based upon years of experience.

While the community is accomplishing the physical challenges of addressing needs such as clean water, better access roads, health classes, etc., we are constantly keeping vigil that the components of the process are being accomplished. The focus in each step of the process is the community itself and what is happening among the members of the community. The focus is not the development worker or his/her organization and what they can accomplish.

Here is one last note before discussing the process of development that we are striving to see happen in the community. Every community is going through development. We cannot assume that we are coming into a vacuum. We also best assume that we are not coming in as "saviors" to the villagers' problems. They already have developed ways to handle their problems. Some may seem to be negative development or so slow that it is hard to measure. Also, if they need a "savior," it is dangerous for us to point to ourselves. We should come alongside them as friends and partners in their efforts at development and, in the process, point them to the true Savior they need to be looking toward and dependent upon: Jesus.

The basic steps to the community development/Kingdom development process are:

1. The Community Becomes More Aware and Identifies Problems – The first step in the process is to raise the community's awareness regarding what problems face them and the identification of those problems. They of course can already identify many of their problems without our help. However, our goal is to work with them in such a way that people communicate with each other and are able to express their views and concerns so that the whole community begins to see a more complete picture. During this step in the process, we are usually surprised by the hidden problems that often surface. Generally one or two groups (such as women, youth, single-households, etc.) who are typically marginalized in the existing power structures have a chance to voice their concerns and be heard. Finding ways that the community voices and hears the whole set of problems is often an eye-opening time for most of the members of that community. It helps build empathy and community when all see the bigger picture. Based upon the awareness generated, the community begins to work together to identify the particular problems facing them. The development worker uses various tools at this stage to begin getting the people working and thinking together to come up with a comprehensive list of problems they see. No problem is too small or too large to consider. The idea

here is not analyzing (this is in the next step) but identification. Sometimes at this stage in the process, the development worker is tempted to disavow some of the problems identified as "trivial" or "too massive" to address. However, in many cases these problems are the ones that communities eventually decide to act upon. It is much better to let them dream and be exhaustive in their identification time because it may lead to a seemingly trivial, massive, or even hidden problem that becomes their first project. After all, it is their identification of problems, not ours.

2. The Community Analyzes and Prioritizes the Problems – Next, based upon the problems that are identified, the development worker begins to use tools to help the community analyze their problems. This analysis may take the form of placing them into categories such as feasible problems to handle, biophysical classification, focus group specific, etc. In this stage we are hoping to see the community begin to narrow down its focus and determine/set some priorities as to which problems are the most critical to the immediate development of the community. We are also helping them to slowly narrow down to a few problems (with corresponding projects) that are feasible, doable, and relatively easy to address within a short period of time. Problem analysis helps the community to look at each problem from a number of different angles and "triangulate." Triangulation refers to the method of looking at something in multiple ways in order to gain better insight and validation. Prioritizing helps the community to begin to narrow

its focus and move toward one initial problem to address.

3. The Community Identifies and Prioritizes Solutions – After problems are identified, initially analyzed, and in some way prioritized, the goal is to lead the community in exercises focused on developing possible solutions to the highest priority problems. At this stage no solution is too trivial or too large for consideration. Brainstorming and creativity should be encouraged among the group. People should not be corrected or told their ideas are not realistic, especially by the development worker. Using good communication and analysis tools at this stage gives the power to the local people. My experience has been that people, when given this opportunity, can come up with some amazing possibilities. After the group has discussed multiple solutions to a few priority problems, they then begin to narrow their focus to one priority problem and one priority solution. They need to save/record all of the work they have done in order to make a comprehensive plan. However, they will start with one problem and one solution in order to get through a whole cycle of problem solving in the development process. Ideally, we would like them to also begin with something that is achievable in a relatively realistic time so that they can see success and results regarding their efforts. Eventually, they will develop and implement a comprehensive plan, but the initial plan is usually limited to one to two items in order to keep it simple and doable. Additionally, the planning tool for this step is also kept simple. The community can make it more elaborate and comprehensive later as they gain skills and

confidence in the development process.

4. The Community Develops and Implements Their Plan – At this stage, the community has identified a number of problems and prioritized which one they want to attack first. They also have explored a number of solutions to that problem and developed a plan of action that is within their power to implement given a reasonable period of time. They have analyzed the resources needed to accomplish the task and made assignments according to what needs to be done, who will do it, when it needs to be completed, and what is needed (resources) to accomplish the task. A simple action plan that is agreed upon by the community can then be documented and posted in a public place in the community such as a town hall, village square, etc.

5. The Community Monitors, Evaluates, Celebrates, and Moves On to the Next Problem – The temptation at this point is for the development worker to now jump in and begin "running" the project by doing all the monitoring and evaluation. However, we need to continue to remember that it is their development and their project, not ours. At any point in the process when we take the project out of their hands, it ceases to belong to the community and becomes ours. In doing this, we will defeat the main goal of community development. If the community is going to move on to bigger and better projects in the future, they need the skills and experience at all of these stages of the development process. If we monitor, we should monitor ourselves

as to how well we have helped them implement this process as well as develop the necessary capabilities, capacities, interdependency, confidence, and Christ-likeness to become a better community. We should encourage the community to celebrate their victories. Also, we should encourage them to move on to other problems and projects utilizing the new skills that they have learned. Our celebration as development workers comes from seeing good projects accomplished by the community because they have applied a good process in getting there. Not only do they gain a "project," but also they gain the ability to do more projects and to begin taking charge, in confidence, of their further developmental needs.

Graphically, the five-step process described above would look something like this:

Figure 2 – The community development process

How Long Should the Process Take?

This is a good question and a hard one to answer with a "one size fits all" rule. Therefore, I will respond by describing our experience. Adding to this, I have found similar experiences of other organizations doing the same type of development work.

Typically, we stay with a community for a three to five year period depending upon response and needs. Within that time frame, we are able to go through three to five "cycles" of the development process which translates into three to five priority problems addressed with corresponding projects that are implemented to solve those problems. Typically, it takes three to six months to introduce ourselves to the community and build trust to the point that we can use the development tools and get to the identification of the first project to be implemented. After we have gone through the development process the first time, it is generally easier to do the second time and increasingly less difficult in subsequent applications of the process.

In the first cycle, we are heavily involved with leading and teaching the community the skills and art of the development process. In the second cycle, we are already beginning to transfer the leadership and initiative to local people. By the time we reach the third, fourth, and fifth cycles (if we stay that long), the whole process is pretty much being led by the community itself.

In the three to five year time frame that we commit to the community, there are three phases that our program consciously goes through:

(1) Entry, (2) Implementation, and (3) Exit. The reason I say "three to five years" is that we (in principle) come up with a set of pre-determined exit indicators that serve to help us assess when our work within a particular community is ready for phasing out. The exit indicators are more focused on what processes we accomplished and less focused on how the community "performed." Some common exit indicators would include factors such as:

1. The community completed "x" number of development cycles.

2. There was an "x" percentage of success in the development projects attempted by the community.

3. The community gained "x" number of new skills needed to further their development.

4. The community made "x" number of new network linkages with outside organizations/agencies.

5. The community now has regularly scheduled meetings "x" number of times per week/month to address issues and problems in the community.

6. The community has recognized "x" number of newly emerging leaders in their development work.

7. The community has "x" number of people that have spiritually transformed lives.

8. The community has and is showing Christ-likeness by

_____.

The Process Expanded

If we were to expand the process graphically to show it as a growing process over a three to five year period along with corresponding phases, it would look something like this:

Figure 3. The development process expanded with phases

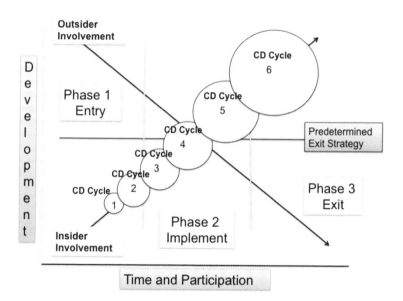

In the expanded process, the decreasing role of the outsider (development worker) is seen as indirectly proportional to the increasing role and involvement of the insiders or community. Each of the circles above represents the previously discussed five-stage development process. The cycles are increasing in size and moving upwards to indicate the increasing complexity of problems addressed and projects taken on by the local community.

Notice the pre-determined exit strategy baseline. This is the "time frame" or better "performance indicator line" which we set in order to have some gauge as to when our work is ready to phase out within a particular community. Notice in the above diagram, the community has passed through five or six development cycles when the exit baseline is crossed. The community's successful completion of this number of development cycles would give us some indication that they are ready to move on by themselves to bigger and better projects and we are needing to phase down our work with them.

The three phases above correspond to our three phases discussed, namely entry, implementation, and phasing out. Ideally, by the time the community is involved in the larger cycles of the development process (phases 2 and 3 above), they no longer need the services/guidance of the development worker and we then can move on to other communities. This is the fulfillment of an old Chinese proverb that states, "But of the best leaders, when their work is accomplished, their work is done, the people all remark, 'We have done it ourselves.'"

Distinguishing Between Relief and Development

At this point, a distinction should be made between relief and development strategies. While both are crucial in responding to human needs around the world, in this book, we are primarily referring to developmental work.

Generally, human needs ministries and development work are broken down into two broad categories. These categories are based upon the type of need addressed and though not fixed, serve as the foundational ethos as to how one approaches a particular potential problem or need. A complete development organization and/or worker will tend to look at both of these categories and act accordingly as needed per given situation.

1. Acute Human Needs Problems – These needs arise from disaster events such as wars, famine, earthquakes, floods, etc., and are highly unpredictable as to when or where they will happen. They are generally short-term and life threatening. Immediate response (within the first 48 to 72 hours) is critical to saving lives and the effectiveness of the program. They can and do open windows for ministry usually of a shorter duration period than chronic needs. They are generally dealt with through emergency relief/disaster response. Acute crises usually refers to a brief period of time in which food, and/or other needed resources may need to be distributed or appropriate aid given. Programs/ministries addressing these issues are generally described as "relief" ministries.

2. Chronic Human Needs Problems – These problems include human suffering due to hunger, poverty, poor health, etc., and are generally long-term and often massive in proportion. Because the problems causing chronic suffering are deeply rooted in human so-

cieties and cultures, they usually require long-term, transformational, education-based solutions. They generally seek to transform the things within the community that are the causative agents of the problems being addressed. Thus, programs/ministries addressing these issues are termed "developmental" or "transformational."

Thus, acute needs are generally addressed through disaster relief strategies and programs. These can be in the form of responding to a disaster, mitigation of potential disasters, management of a disaster response and recovery/rehabilitation. On the other hand, chronic needs are addressed through developmental strategies. These can range from work in food security, primary health care, water/sanitation, education, microfinance/microenterprise, or general community development. Both focuses are needed and valid. In many cases, good disaster response can transition and lead to good development projects (if done correctly and with the purpose to do so). Again, the focus of this book is community development that addresses the longer-term, chronic problems faced by a community.

The Sliding Scale of Development

When we think about community development, different ideas and concepts come to mind. Some people think about projects: We help the community develop by doing projects for or with the community that helps them with their development. On the other side, some people think about the process: We work with the community to affect better processes whereby the community makes the changes.

Both are probably two sides of the same coin or more aptly, two sides of what I call a sliding scale of development. On one side, you have pure community development whereby the development change agent acts as a facilitator and resists entering into the community's problems with any resources. They rely on getting communities organized and empowering communities to solve their own problems with their own resources.

On the other side, you have the project-oriented person who sees problems, enters into those problems, and engages both with their time and efforts as well as outside resources to solve the identified problems. While both approaches probably represent the two extremes (pure community development versus pure project implementation), there are a wide variety of approaches that fall somewhere in-between these two. And, from experience, most development organizations and workers honestly fall somewhere along this sliding scale.

Figure 4. The sliding scale of developmental approaches

THE SLIDING SCALE OF DEVELOPMENT

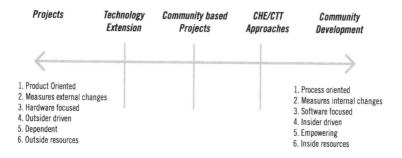

All of these approaches can be successful, or they can be detrimental as well. Much depends on the person/organization implementing the development: ethos, training, personality, gifting, etc. A lot also depends upon the host community: past experiences in development, worldview, dependency tendencies, view of/experience with outsiders, etc.

When I look at the sliding scale in relation to my own gifting and preferences, I tend to fall more towards the pure community development side. I have a strong proclivity towards helping people help themselves and them doing this with largely their own resources. I believe that this is the more sustainable way to development as well as the best way to guard against issues such as dependency and unhealthy relationships. I also tend to think this is more in line with the Bible and God's plan for people and communities.

Nevertheless, I do not argue that there are some great examples of project-based development programs that have made a difference as well. Therefore, I will not be quick to judge one over the other. The majority of development workers probably fall somewhere between the two poles and in reality, slide back and forth in their approaches due to the particular situation and what it calls for at the time. I do think we tend to return to our particular bias, such as myself leaning heavily towards the purer community development side, but I think we slide back and forth in our approaches and implementation of development programs/projects depending upon particular needs.

Initial Actions at Point of Entry

So we have entered into the community. We have chosen our area to work. We know who we are and what are targets are as well as our limitations. We have developed initial relationships and have done some trust building to the point that we are fairly sure which individuals and which core group we will begin with in our community development project. The rest should be easy, right?

At the point of getting to the community and launching our program, we now need to communicate even better than before. On a macro side, we have obtained the blessings of government leaders and other powerbrokers to be in a particular community and at a particular level. However, rather than being finished with our work, the real work is only beginning.

How do we engage in dialog with individuals and communities in a way that addresses their deepest felt needs? How do we wade through the myriad of felt needs and determine real needs? How do we make sure that this process is not ours or driven by our organizational ethos and biases? How do we know that what we will be discussing is truly what the community wants to see happen? How do we ensure that the whole community is represented and not just one or two strong voices are heard in the process?

In community development work, thankfully we have a large toolbox filled with useful tools to help us in our journey. The next few chapters will discuss these tools in a way that relates each of them to a particular step within the community development process. As we study them, remember that most of these tools are multi-functional and can be used at different steps in the process than what I have described here. Also, as we unpack these tools, we need to remember that the tools are not the focus of our community development efforts. Our focus is getting people to communicate openly and work together to solve their problems. The tools presented here are simply tools.

The Size of a Community Meeting

Often the question comes up as to what is the ideal size for a community meeting. In reality, we have very little control over this. In a true community meeting, it is open for all members of the community to attend and participate. In some places, we have started with over 300 people. This is a difficult group size to handle and to truly get good interaction and participation. Typically, the first few community meetings are fairly large but they begin to lessen in terms of participants as time goes on.

However many people show up for our meetings, we still try to get them into small group settings of five to ten people per group. This allows for lively discussion and facilitates participation by all. Therefore, if 300 show up for our initial community meetings, during discussion and interaction time where we begin applying these tools, we might look at breaking them into 30 groups of 10 people per group. Each group would begin using the same tools and reporting by smaller groups back to the larger group as a whole which should bring about some valuable discussion and insights to the community. It also could be a way for the community to see some hidden problems or it might be a good way for the community to validate some of its priority problems. For instance, what if you had 30 groups talking about the village problems and 28 of them identified a good source of drinking water as one of their priority needs?

Again, our experience has shown that involvement and participation will shrink a bit from the initial meetings and we will eventually begin to separate into manageable groups in relation to size and affinity. In some cases, special focus groups will form around things such as gender, age, and even occupation/interests. None of these are bad as long as their findings/ideas are brought back and tempered with the overall community's goals and priorities.

What Should We Do in a Community Meeting?

Another common question is what the contents of a community meeting should be, especially the first one. I would encourage you to plan ahead and make the meeting fun and interesting. Of course we want to get to the development tools, but we should take some time especially in the first meetings to introduce ourselves and get to know one another. Icebreakers, depending on cultural appropriateness, are often a good place to start. Simple games that get people moving and interacting or even simple songs are usually a fun way to begin. We usually use songs that have motions. This gets people up and moving and generates a relaxed feeling among the group.

A typical first meeting might include (but not be limited to):

1. Icebreakers

2. Group and individual introductions (can use games here)

3. An introduction to who we are (organizational-wise), why we are meeting, and what we hope to accomplish. Depending on the situation, we might also want to share our approval process for working in their community and/or our credentials

4. Some type of response from the leader(s) of the group

5. Questions and answers to put the local people at ease

6. Maybe beginning to use the first tools in our toolkit

7. Prayer/asking God's blessings on our endeavors. This may be tricky depending on the local people and their faith, but I have found most communities and people to be at the least respectful of the request for help from a power higher than ourselves

8. Discussion of a memorandum of understanding or agreement (MOU/MOA) for us working in the community might be discussed at this time. Clear-cut expectations of all parties as we start is usually a good point to begin. While these are not legally binding in most cases, it helps to have a reference point to come back to when things begin to go awry (for either the outsider or the insider). A sample of an MOU made with one community in Central Asia by a good development worker can be found in Appendix 2.

Remember, from the very first meeting, you are setting patterns of how they will accept, reject, or even embrace the development process. Also, the more you do for people, the more they will let you do. Our goal as development workers is to facilitate the process, not run it. Therefore, as soon as possible, we should be getting local participants involved in leading the meetings, using the tools, and taking charge of the discussions. A general rule of thumb is that the community participants should be talking/discussing 80% of the time and we should only be speaking 20%.

Things to Remember:

As we close this chapter, I would like to review a couple of key points. Even though I've already discussed much of what follows, it bears repeating.

1. The community is the focus, not us – If we review the development cycle and the stages involved, we will clearly see that the word "community" is prevalent. This is because the process, projects, and ensuing development belongs to the community, not us. We should always keep this in mind as we work in development work. Whose development is it? Whose planning? Whose priority setting? Whose responsibility for taking action? Sustainability begins when people take ownership of their problems and processes to solve those problems. We need to remember that we are catalysts at best in the process be-

cause in the end, it is the community that has to catch the vision and do the work.

2. Initial projects and plans need to be simple, feasible, and attainable within a reasonable period of time – No doubt, people and communities are capable of coming up with great ideas and elaborate plans for their development. However, in the initial stages, we are looking to guide them to something that is fairly simple to work on as their first project. For instance, when prioritizing their problems, they may include things such as electrification of the village. While this would be a needed project for their development, it generally would be a complex one that would possibly require years of work to see accomplished. If the initial problem they work on is too complex and takes too long to solve, people may lose interest in the process and abandon it altogether. It is not that the process was faulty, it is just too hard to wait a long time for results especially for the poorer communities. Moreover, failure at this initial point due to an overreaching project can compound a defeatist attitude that the community may already have. We do want to help communities dream big and grow the ability to handle even its most complex problems. However, our experience has been to start simple and grow into the more complex problems.

3. Any problem the community chooses to work on will accomplish our goals for development, so let them choose – In keeping with number 2 above, keep it simple initially. We need to remember that

any project/problem chosen by the community to work on can get us towards the developmental goals of taking the community through the development cycle. Thus, it is important to lean heavily on what the community identifies as its priority. Remember, their goal is projects leading to good development. Our goal is "how" they get to the point of deciding on and implementing their projects and the abilities and motivation developed to begin reaching out to attack more and more community problems on their own. Our goal is also to help the community begin a succession of development cycles with measurable success that leads them to have confidence and abilities to deal with more complex problems.

4. The evaluation of our success is not on the quality or quantity of projects completed – We want to see good projects and a good number in the community. However, our primary self-evaluation is how well we built capabilities, capacities, confidence, community, and Christ-likeness in the people with whom we worked.

Chapter Summary

• Community development is a process in which communities enter to be able to become better at meeting their own needs. Kingdom development is community development with an eternal focus.

• The measure of success for community development is more about what happens in the lives of the community members and collective group. It is not about our organizational goals or how well we do our work, but rather how well the community comes together to solve their problems.

• From a Kingdom development standpoint, we want to see individuals and communities move toward a lifestyle that is reflective of God's word and plan for people, and we want to see them actively propagating what God has blessed them with for eternal purposes.

Chapter 6
Step One Tools: The Community Becomes More Aware and Identifies Problems

As stated earlier, in the first step of the community development process, our goal as development workers is to begin to engage the community in dialogue in a way that raises awareness of community issues as well as leads toward identifying problems. This is a discovery phase not only for the outsider but also for the insiders as well. Adequate time should be given to this step and initial observations should be thoroughly discussed to reveal deeper, hidden feelings and values of the host community.

Remember that this initial step and its corresponding tools are the initial gateways into the community. This is a time of building relationships with the community, and a crucial time for trust building or breaking. The good development worker keeps in the forefront that he/she is the outsider only helping and/or facilitating the development process. The awareness and identification of the community's problems belong to the community, not the outsider. This will bear much weight later on when we come to the time of solution identification and resource allocation. If we allow this to truly be a community owned process, it must start here where the community takes ownership and leads in the discussion of its issues.

The tools of community awareness
and problem identification

1. Situational/trend analysis – In a situational analysis, we usually gather the community in a meeting setting to begin discussing community resources and situations in the past, in the present, and what they think will happen in the future. This is a good tool to gain insight into how the community perceives itself and its future. For instance, we might ask them to discuss or even map out what the community was like 20 years ago, what is like today, and what it will be like 20 years from now in relation to topics such as food supply, water, jobs, soil fertility, health, etc. We need to remember that these are not scientifically quantitative answers but rather descriptions and perceptions from the community's standpoint that will give us a picture or trend of what they believe is happening. It also helps them begin to discuss issues, voice ideas among themselves, and heighten the community awareness of what everyone else thinks is going on in the community. A typical situational analysis might look something like this:

Figure 5. A Simple Community Situational Analyses

ITEM	20 YEARS AGO	TODAY	20 YEARS FROM NOW
FOOD	⬆	⬌	⬇
WATER	⬌	⬌	⬇
HEALTH	⬇	⬆	⬌
INCOME	⬇	⬌	⬇
FORESTS	⬆	⬇	⬇

A simple set of arrow indicators can be used per cell to visually illustrate the group's perception. We use "up" arrows to indicate an increase, "down" arrows to indicate a decrease and "horizontal" arrows to indicate no change. For example, in the food security row, the group might place an up arrow under the "20 Years Ago" column, a sideways arrow in the "Today" column and a down arrow in the "20 Years from Now" column. This would indicate that they perceive food security as something that is worsening over time. This tool helps us see the trends that the community perceives to be true. In the case above, it looks as if the community has a pretty negative view about the future. This tool also might help the community to begin to identify some of the priority problems facing them.

2. Focus Group discussions – When the community begins to come together, sometimes there are sub-groups that naturally break out from the larger group. Some of these might be women groups, youth groups, farmer groups, etc., who have special interests in particular problems. For instance, in one village where we worked, the main meeting naturally segmented into sub-groups who had their own special needs. The male farmers (who were the decision makers) were interested in livestock and new crops that they might grow. The majority of the women were more interested in health classes (including birth control), a new source of drinking water (because they hauled the water that was a long way to the source), and small income-generating projects. The young people were interested in getting a simple sports facility going for the village. We asked them to meet in their main interest group, develop a list of their priority needs/concerns, and then present them together along with the other focus groups back to the whole community. Not every problem/agenda item could be addressed immediately, but it was a good place to start where people heard a wide variety of concerns but also could see the overall needs of the village.

3. Historical Timelines – A historical timeline maps out the major events that have happened in the life of the community. This tells us a lot about the community, their struggles, and hopefully their victories. It usually creates a lively discussion and good community building as people remember together significant events in their history.

This can be done orally or visually. In some cases, you might ask the oldest person in the meeting to tell the history of the village to the group. In other cases, you might produce a visual timeline (on paper, on the ground, etc.) of events. It is not unusual for the community not to be able to provide exact dates. But remember, we are looking for significant events and not a historically certifiable document. People remembering, verbalizing, or even visualizing their history can lead to the discovery of many important things. For instance, if you were to engage in dialogue with a community and ascertain with their village history as seen in Figure 5, you might conclude that the community constantly thinks about water (or lack thereof) and possibly food and food security. You can also see that there are some positive things that the community is proud of such as their education, water wells, and their community center.

Figure 6. A sample simple village time line of major events

TIME LINE EXAMPLE – VILLAGE ORAL HISTORY

1916-17 –   Drought

1936 –   Drought, school started in cowshed, cholera breakout

1939 –   Drought

1956 –   Drought, supply of rice from other states

1960 –   Primary school set up

1962 –   Land settlement

1964 –   Major pest attack

1965 –   Drought, milk and rice provided by government

1972 –   Drought, distribution of land deeds, construction of road by local government

1975-78 –   Four years drought

1980 –   Drought

1988 –   Installation of tube wells

1994 –   Construction of community center

1996 –   Drought

4. Situational Mapping – This is one of our favorite awareness tools and is usually enthusiastically accepted by the local community. In this exercise, we ask the community to come up with a visual map of their community. We might describe it as if they were a bird flying over their village. What would it look like? They could do this on the ground. In most cases, we try and provide large sheets of paper and

writing implements so that they can actually make a map. In less literate groups, this might take a little longer but we have found even illiterates to be very creative when they grasp the exercise and what they need to do. In making a map of their community, we encourage them to include major landmarks such as roads, bodies of water, mountains, and houses/buildings. We also encourage them to draw the pictures of what the actual situation is today complete with the problems they perceive. This tool, when combined with some later tools, is useful in developing a plan for addressing the community problems.

Figure 7. A Sample Situational Map

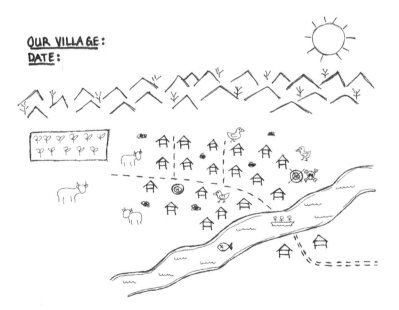

5. Appreciative Inquiry – Appreciative Inquiry or "AI" is usually promoted as a total approach for community development. It is seen

as an alternative to a problem solving approach (which is the basis of this book) and works from the premise that it is best to start with the positive aspects in a community and not the problematic ones. It helps the community recognize and celebrate the good things within the community and build from there instead of starting with the negative such as the problems. Some development workers feel that when we start with the problems, we reinforce the negative stereotypes of under-developed people and communities as "failures" and thus foster poor self worth, dependency on outsiders, and a savior/needing deliverance mentality.

AI begins with seeking the good things in the community. This can be done via asking a series of questions such as:

- *What do you like about your community?*
- *Tell me the good things that have happened in your community?*
- *Why do you like living here?*
- *What are you proud about in relation to your community?*
- *What is your community famous for?*

I personally like this approach and have found it to be helpful especially in the first few steps of the community development cycle. It can be very useful in trust building and entry into a community. It shows respect and interest in their community and does not set the community development worker up as the provider of development to the community.

However, I have found the AI approach to be somewhat lacking when we move deeper into the development process. What we typically find is that even though most communities are proud of and like the place they live, they also see the problems and issues. In a development process, we eventually get back to the need of basic problem solving. The AI framework does not provide well for this, in my experience. I do encourage its use though in the early stages of the development cycle.

6. Village Transects or Walks – Sometimes, a simple field trip whereby a group of community representatives walk around the village and visually/verbally identify problems is a useful tool. This is usually only good for a one-time exercise but can help the whole group to see the problems first hand. Also, it can lead to the "discovery" of hidden problems as the group members begin to discuss issues among themselves. This is a good tool but one that should not be overused.

7. Vision Mapping – One of the key tools we use for problem identification is called community vision mapping. Combined with the situational map, vision mapping can be an excellent tool in determining people's perceptions of the problems in a community. It usually is a fun tool as well that is a highlight of our village meetings. In this exercise, we help the village to dream and draw a map (similar to the situational map) of what their ideal village would look like. In other words, if they could have a "perfect village," what would it in-

clude? We ask them to use the same basic format of the situational map (for comparison purposes) drawing the same reference points such as roads, bodies of water, etc. However, the difference in this map is that they draw the community as if all the problems were solved and their community was now an ideal community.

Figure 8. A Sample Community Vision Map

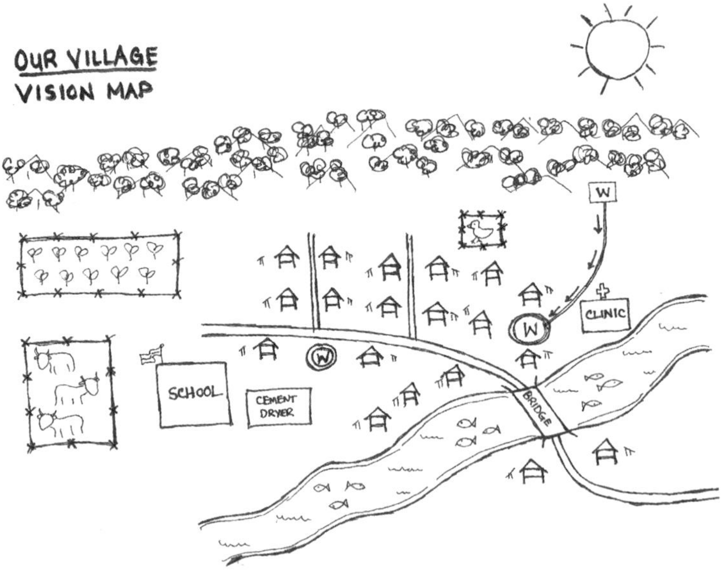

By comparing the situational map and vision map, the community can identify problems that they need to begin working on in order to see development of their community take place. The vision map allows them to dream and gives us a key insight into their dreams and hopes for a better life. We encourage the community to keep this map and refer back to it from time to time in order to see their progress in achieving their goals. In many instances, communities will actually post this map in a public place such as a community meeting hall or village offices and use it as a visual reminder of their goals.

8. Community Surveys – Surveys (formal or informal) can be used in a group meeting to help identify existing problems. However, since this is more individual and less group participation oriented, we choose to use these sparingly. Notes regarding community surveying are attached in Appendix 3.

9. Services/Opportunities Mapping – Another way of enabling a community to visualize its situation and raise awareness of issues is to use a services and opportunities map. This is not meant to be a "to scale" map but simply a reflection of where the community sees itself in respect to access to basic services. Generally we would place the community at the center of the diagram and then ask, "Where is/where do you go for _____. How far away is it from your community?"

This tool gives us a general picture of services available and not easily available to a community. It also might help us to begin to identify some opportunities for initial projects.

Figure 9. A Sample Services/Opportunity Map for a Village

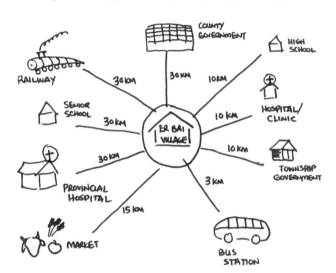

Chapter Summary

• Several good tools can help us begin to identify issues and potential in the community.

• The good development worker keeps in the forefront that he/she is the outsider and is only helping and/or facilitating the development process.

• The awareness and identification of the community's problems belong to the community, not the outsider.

• The best way to learn which tools are best in your community is to begin using them.

Chapter 7
Step Two Tools: The Community Analyzes and Prioritizes the Problems

The second step in the community development process sees the community moving from a heightened awareness of community issues and particular problem identification to analyzing the emerging problems. The community development worker continues in a facilitating and learning mode, making sure not to cut off the community's analysis of problems identified. Remember, it is their problem(s), not ours. They must be the ones to think through them. Also keep in mind that we are at best visitors in the community and there are many issues that we cannot understand.

The tools of community problem analysis

1. Pair-wise Ranking – It is necessary to look at the identified problems from different angles. One way to do this is to consider the problems identified based on their relative importance when compared against each other. This allows the community to look and evaluate each individual problem as a one-on-one comparison against each other problem. We can do this by using a tool called pair-wise ranking. While it is a ranking tool (somewhat quantitative), it is also a good tool to facilitate the community openly discussing their problems that can

be very revealing.

With this tool, we develop a grid that allows the community to compare issues in a head-to-head manner. For instance, if they have identified four or five primary problems, a simple grid where each of the problems is placed in a row and a column can facilitate this comparison. They can then choose which is more important or urgent to the community such as "lack of water" over "income." Remember, this is their perception of their needs/problems. It is not ours. We might disagree with their analysis but in the end, it is more important that the process and information comes from and belongs to them.

When the grid is developed, there will be some empty cells (e.g. where the rows and columns overlap) due to the fact that we only want a one-time one-on-one comparison between items being compared. When the grid is completed and the community has chosen their priorities, they can use symbols or any method of their choosing to illustrate their results. The results can then serve as a good conversation centerpiece where the community discusses back and forth the results.

A sample pair-wise ranking tool is presented as follows:

Figure 10. An Example of a Pair-Wise Ranking of Community Problems

PROBLEM	LACK OF FOOD	LACK OF WATER	LACK OF HEALTH CARE	LACK OF INCOME	LACK OF FORESTS	RESULT
LACK OF FOOD	X	(water)	(food)	(food)	(food)	3
LACK OF WATER	X	X	(water)	(water)	(water)	4
LACK OF HEALTH CARE	X	X	X	(health)	(health)	2
LACK OF INCOME	X	X	X	X	(income)	1
LACK OF FORESTS	X	X	X	X	X	Ø

In the above tool, each identified problem is ranked against each other problem by the community. The problems are placed in rows and then tiers and then ranked one at a time against each other and only once. In the case above, the container symbol represents water, the head of wheat represents food, the syringe and needle represent health care and the "peso" symbol represents income. In the example, the communities perception of which problem is most serious comes out to be: water > food > health concerns > income > forests (natural resources).

2. Calendaring – Another way to look at the problems is through

the lens of seasons or a calendar. This will help the community to possibly see trends in the problems (over time, due to seasons, etc.) and also be useful in the action planning time later on. It can also help visualize the priority of the problem in terms of the year's labor framework. This is very important for rural communities whose lives are planned around agriculture cycles and seasons. Also, trends of climate/weather may give extra insight to the community's problem such as "poor roads" identified as a high priority during times such rainy season, etc. Another thing that often happens during the use of this tool is that community members begin to make connections between problems. For example, the road situation is worse in the rainy season and this contributes to an increase in health problems because residents cannot get to the doctor. In short, they begin to see the "web" of causes and effects with their community problems.

Figure 11. A Typical Calendaring of Problems

PROBLEM	JAN	FEB	MAR	APR	MAY	JUN	JUL	AUG	SEP	OCT	NOV	DEC
LOW FOOD	HIGH	HIGH	HIGH	MED	LOW	LOW	LOW	MED	LOW	LOW	LOW	MED
LOW WATER	HIGH	HIGH	HIGH	HIGH	HIGH	HIGH	HIGH	HIGH	HIGH	HIGH	HIGH	HIGH
LOW HEALTH	LOW	LOW	MED	MED	HIGH	HIGH	MED	MED	HIGH	HIGH	MED	LOW
LOW INCOME	HIGH	HIGH	HIGH	MED	LOW	LOW	LOW	MED	LOW	LOW	MED	MED
LOW FORESTS	HIGH	HIGH	HIGH	HIGH	HIGH	HIGH	HIGH	HIGH	HIGH	HIGH	HIGH	HIGH

KEY:

"HIGH" = High incidence of problem stated

"MED" = Medium incidence of problem stated

"LOW" = Low incidence of problem stated

In the above calendar, the village can see patterns of problems. For instance, when food supply is low (indicated by a "high" incidence of the problem), income is low as well. Conversely, food and income are more available in the rainy seasons (May to July and September to November) because that is when food is being produced. Income is higher because in most rural communities, excess food produced is translated into income. On the other hand, a reverse trend for health is seen. When the rainy season comes, so do the major diseases such as malaria, cholera, and dysentery. In the case above, lack of water and disappearing forests are seen as constantly high problems.

3. Cause and Effect Analysis (Problem Tree) – Another useful tool in looking at a problem from different angles is the cause/effect analysis or the "problem tree." The goal in this exercise is for the community to discuss and formulate ideas as to what the "causes" are behind a particular problem and the "effects" based upon each cause. We usually describe it as a tree with the "causes" being the roots and the "effects" being the fruits. We can actually have the community draw a tree for visualization purposes and then write the main problem being discussed in the trunk area. They then begin brainstorming and placing

the causes of this particular problem in the rooting area. Next they will begin drawing the fruits or effects in the branches area. For instance, they may identify "lack of water" as a main problem (the tree trunk). The roots (causes) might then be labeled "no good source," "sources too far from the village," "poor water quality," "insufficient supply," "dry season," etc. After identifying the main problem and most of the root causes, they would then begin brainstorming and recording what the effects or "fruits" are that occur in the community as a result of the problem. Using the above example they might say, "more work for the women – long haul," "sick children," "high cost to buy water," "wasted time standing in line to wait for water," etc. Thus, their problem tree for lack of water might look as follows:

Figure 12. The Problem Tree Exercise

Cause and effect tools such as the problem tree can be used on all the priority problems that the village identifies. Not only does it show information about the problem, but it also helps the community to begin thinking about the practicality (or impracticality) of addressing certain problems they list. For instance, one cause of the lack of water would be dry season when there is less water available. It may become clear that for many of the causes it is impractical to find a solution. Another advantage of the problem tree tool is that it provides a way to identify where the community will expend its energies in solving a particular problem. We often ask the community if they had a tree that was sick, what would they treat: the fruit or the roots? They would answer, "The roots, of course." We then would equate this to the problems in the village. If the "roots" are the causes and the "fruits" are the effects, which ones should we try and find solutions for, the causes or the effects?

4. Labor Mapping – Another analysis tool that is useful in some situations is making a labor map. Given that some problems identified by the community might rank equal in terms of priority, a simple labor map might help sway a decision as to which problem would be the wisest to tackle first. Labor maps can be long-term and combined with a calendar-type tool to show work required over time. A labor map could be required for each problem identified (e.g. labor required to build a water system versus labor required to start some type of new agriculture project).

Another type of labor map would be a daily map of existing labor requirements with the addition of the labor required by the new project. It is sometimes helpful in labor mapping to separate labor by gender and age. In other words, preparing a labor map breaking out the role of men, women, and children. In many cases, communities become animated (especially the women) when labor roles and time spent is visualized.

Chapter Summary

• There are many good tools to help us with problem analysis.

• However, remember this: we are at best visitors in the community and there are many issues that we cannot understand.

Chapter 8
Step Three Tools: The Community Identifies and Prioritizes Solutions

After identifying the problems in a community using the tools discussed and prioritizing the problems of the community, we now move to solution identification. Ideally, through our meeting times and interaction as a community, we might have even narrowed down our priority to one particular problem that the village sees as important and solvable. We will eventually be developing a comprehensive development plan based upon all the knowledge gleaned, but formulating an initial project that solves a problem and takes the community through the cycle of development the first time is critical. That is why we try to help them move toward a simple yet achievable first project. Any problem/project they choose to work on is in theory acceptable. Our main goal as development workers is to complete the whole cycle of development in a relatively short time with some success.

The tools we use for solution identification build upon the tools we have already completed, such as the example given in the problem tree analysis exercise. This can be elaborated on with group discussion/ solution brainstorming. A resource analysis via a Venn diagram can also help the community to see how practical the proposed solutions really are.

Tools for community identification
and prioritization of solutions

1. Solution identification using the problem tree – At this stage in the process, we can take the problem tree analysis done by each group and have them brainstorm about possible solutions per each cause identified. We should encourage them to identify as many solutions as they can for each cause and discuss the possibilities of each of those solutions. In most cases, patterns begin to emerge as groups see that there are some causes that they probably cannot find a solution for (e.g. lack of water due to dry season – they cannot change the fact that they have a dry season every year). In some cases, they will begin to see a common solution emerge that becomes clear to the group as a viable option to solve the problem (e.g. getting a good water source closer to the village would take care of the women's long haul, give better and more water, improve the health of children, etc.). This is an exciting time when the community working together begins to formulate an idea that will solve their problem.

2. Linking/comparing of situational and vision maps – By comparing the situational map and vision map, the community can identify problems that need to be addressed in order for development of their community to take place. The vision map allows them to dream and gives us a key insight into their dreams and hopes for a better life. We encourage the community to keep this map for future reference

and refer back to it from time to time in order to see their progress in achieving their goals. In many instances, communities will actually post this map in a public place such as a community meeting hall or village office and use it as a visual reminder of their goals.

If we compare the vision map with the situation map prepared earlier by the community, we can identify a number of problems that the community sees. For instance, the improvements made by the community in the vision map example include:

1. *Penned animals and fenced crops*
2. *Improved access road/bridge*
3. *More fish in the river*
4. *Reforested mountains*
5. *A good water system*
6. *Houses with toilets*
7. *A school*
8. *A clinic*
9. *A cement multipurpose pavement (sports, seed drying, etc.)*

3. Resource mapping/Venn diagraming – Let us say that the community has decided to initially begin working on one problem: lack of water in the village. Let us also say that they have identified two to three possible solutions to the problem such as boring a deep well in the village, piping water in from a new source three kilometers away, or setting up a filtration/purification system for the existing water system.

All three of these solutions have pros and cons. Also, there are different villagers supporting each of these solutions. How do they decide?

One tool we use that helps us gauge the feasibility along with the "doability" of a project is resource mapping using a Venn diagram. For each solution, we encourage the community members to make a list of all the resources they will need to accomplish that action. This would include physical items (materials, natural resources, etc.), social items (permissions, endorsements, etc.), and financial items (budget, etc.), among others.

For instance, for the solution "piping water in from a new source three kilometers away", the community might list resources needed to accomplish that particular solution as: 1) three kilometers of pipe, 2) labor to install, 3) technical design, 4) cement and blocks for reservoirs, 5) sand and gravel for the concrete mix, 6) iron reinforcement bars, 7) a truck for hauling and fuel for the truck, 8) permission from the land owner where the source is and permission from all the landowners where we will lay pipe, and 9) government leader endorsement/blessing of the project. We then would ask them to draw a large circle on a sheet of paper. This circle would represent the community and its project – a new water system.

We would then ask them to mark on that paper where each of the needed resources is in relationship to the community. If the community does not have the particular resource already in hand, it would be placed on the outside of the circle (e.g. cement and blocks to construct the reservoir, reinforcement bars, a truck for hauling, etc.). If the community has the resource listed already, they would place it within the circle (e.g. labor, sand and gravel, etc.). If the resource identified is partly in the community and partly outside, they would need to place it on the edge of the circle (e.g. government permission/blessing, technical design, etc.). The above diagram might look something like this:

Figure 13. A Venn Diagram/Resource Analysis of a Village Water System

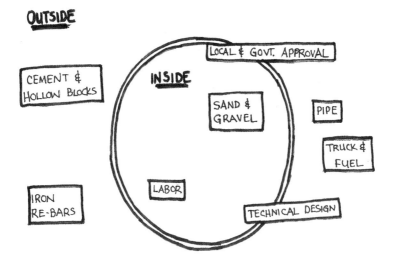

If a resource analysis/Venn diagram is completed for each of the three possible solutions discussed, usually it becomes pretty clear to the community which of the possible solutions is the best one to attempt. Remember, choosing which problem and which solution is their decision. These tools are ways to help them look at the problems and solutions from multiple angles to find the best way that suits their community. Generally speaking, the solutions with more resources "inside" the community than "outside" are the ones that are more feasible and doable because these are resources over which local people have more control.

4. Prioritization tools – At this stage, we will use some of the quantitative tools in order to begin prioritizing which are perceived to be the most immediate threats to the development of the community and thus the highest priority to address. The main goal here is to narrow down the problems to about four or five of the main ones identified by the community. They may have initially identified 20 to 30 problems but many of these are minor and it is hard to address all of them at once. Preference ranking will help us begin to narrow down the focus to a few problems.

a. Ranking – Ranking is probably the simplest form of a quantitative tool. We generally use the classifiers "high", "medium" and "low" to give value to an item or to distinguish between values of numerous items. For instance, in the example of the water problem for the village discussed earlier in this chapter, three possible solutions were chosen to solve the problem: boring a deep well in the village, piping water in from a new source three kilometers away, or setting up a filtration/ purification system for the existing water system. All have their merits and maybe the villagers really are divided as to which course to pursue. A quantitative tool such as ranking can possibly help to break the ice and help the group to move forward on one of the solutions.

Figure 14. A Sample Ranking Exercise

SOLUTION	RANK	
BORE A DEEP WELL	LOW LOW MED HIGH LOW / LOW MED LOW LOW MED MED / MED LOW MED LOW HIGH LOW / MED LOW LOW HIGH LOW HIGH / MED MED / LOW HIGH LOW LOW MED LOW MED	H = 5 M = 10 L = 15
SPRING DEVELOPMENT	HIGH HIGH HIGH HIGH HIGH / MED MED HIGH HIGH MED LOW HIGH / HIGH MED MED HIGH / MED LOW MED LOW HIGH / LOW HIGH HIGH HIGH HIGH / LOW HIGH MED HIGH MED HIGH	H = 16 M = 10 L = 4
FILTRATION SYSTEM	MED HIGH HIGH MED MED MED / MED LOW HIGH HIGH / MED LOW MED MED MED LOW / HIGH LOW MED LOW MED HIGH MED / MED LOW / HIGH MED HIGH MED MED	H = 8 M = 15 L = 7

They would draw a chart (matrix) listing the three possible solutions in one column. They would leave a blank column/cell after each of the proposed solutions and each person in the group would rank the solutions as high, medium or low priority. If there were 30 people in the group, there would be 30 rankings per each solution.

In this case, the solution with the most "highs" would be the one favored by the group. This is of course not scientific and the community can make a different decision in light of the ranking, but it is a tool to help break a deadlock.

b. Scoring – Scoring is similar to ranking and is done basically the same way. However, this method tends to be more useful with a higher literate group. Using the example of choosing between the three solutions to the water problem presented above, a similar matrix is drawn but instead of ranking each intersecting cell with high, medium or low, a number value is assigned to the cell. A scale of 1 to 10 that could be used. If "10" represented the highest level and "1" the lowest, a scoring grid for the previously discussed problem might look something like figure 14.

Figure 15. A Sample Scoring Exercise

SOLUTION	SCORE	

BORE A DEEP WELL	2 4 2 4 3 4 3 4
	  3 2 2 4 2
	2 4 3 3 4 3
	  3 3 4 3 4 2
	4 2 3 3 4 3 3
		AVG= 3

SPRING DEVELOPMENT	10 8 9 10 8 8 10 10 9 8 8 9 8 8 9 9 8 10 9 10 9 8 10 8 9 10 9 10 9 8 10	AVG= 9
FILTRATION SYSTEM	4 4 6 4 5 4 5 5 6 4 5 4 6 5 6 5 4 5 6 5 6 6 4 6 5 6 4 6	AVG= 5

In this case as in the previous one, the higher scoring cells would be indicative of the more preferred solution and the lower scoring cells would be, in theory, the less desired. Again, this tool usually works better with a more formally educated group.

c. Weighting – Weighting is also similar to the two tools above but tends to be a better tool for visual learners. In this method, values are given "weights" or physical properties such as rocks, seeds, or anything locally available that is abundant and small enough to use in the exercise. Each member of the group is given the same number of rocks or seeds and told that each one represents one vote. Thus, if you have a group of 30 people trying to make a decision regarding which of the three solutions to choose, you could draw a similar chart/matrix as to the one described in the first two exercises and then give each person in the group 10 rocks/seeds. I prefer seeds (of the same type) because they are uniform and give a better visual effect to the exercise. Thus each individual would have 10 seeds to place on the matrix for a total of 300 seeds. They would then be asked to place their seeds besides the solution they think is the best one. They can put all 10 seeds by one solution or they can place five seeds by one, three by another and two by the last. It is up to the individual to make his/her choice. To make it confidential, a paper bag or tin can might be placed besides each possible solution and people could "anonymously" place their seeds in their corresponding choice's container. This would remove the pressure and possible loss of face in having to "vote their seeds" in public. However it is done, after the final seed placement, everyone can look and see for themselves the "weight" that they gave to each solution and then determine which one they should pursue based upon the group's preference.

Figure 16. A Sample 10-Seed Method Weighting Exercise

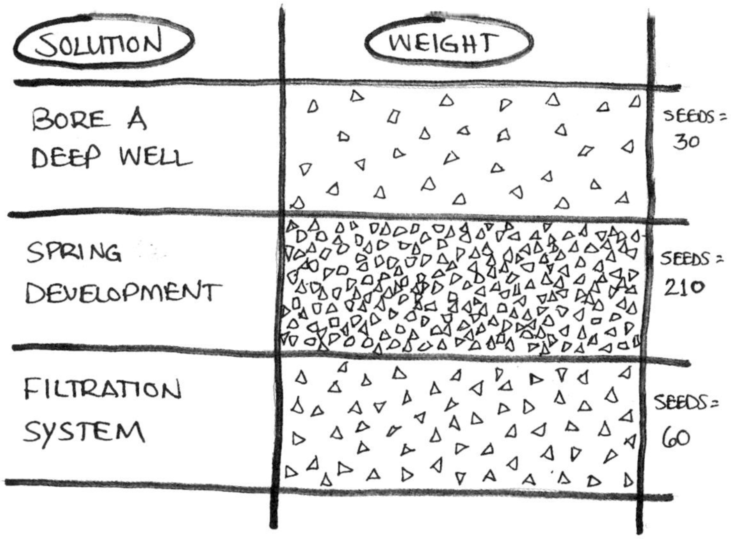

d. Voting – In a situation where appropriate and people are cultur-ally accepting to the idea, a simple voting process of choosing a certain course of action might work. The key to using any one of these quan-titative methods to choose from multiple options is that they should be culturally appropriate and acceptable to the group as a whole. In some cases, systems may need to be devised to respect the privacy of the individual. However, most of these options allow for at least the public display or demonstration of totals so that everyone cannot only hear but see the results.

Chapter Summary

• The tools we use for solution identification build upon the tools we have already completed.

• We will eventually be developing a comprehensive development plan based upon all the knowledge gleaned, but formulating an initial project that solves a problem and takes the community through the cycle of development the first time is critical.

• Any problem/project they choose to work on is in theory acceptable. Our main goal as development workers is to complete the whole cycle of development in a relatively short time with some success.

Chapter 9
Step Four Tools: The Community Develops and Implements Their Plan

By this time, I hope you can see the building progression of where we are going with the development tools. The community has become more aware of their problems and possibly identified some hidden problems. They have analyzed those problems to understand them better and come up with some possible solutions. Moreover, they have prioritized which problem(s) to work on initially and even have a pretty good idea of which solution will work best to solve the particular problem they have chosen to address. Now comes the time to develop an action plan.

After the plan has been completed, we encourage the group to document their decisions and then report back to the whole community. A presentation to the community as a whole and other community leaders will help validate the planned actions of the group and possibly create more excitement and participation.

At the beginning of the process, we start with a large group but as we go along, there will be a number to drop out or just not participate. When the core develops their first plan and project, new community interest is generated and those who previously left the group may rejoin. Also, presenting the plan to the community as a whole increases ownership of the project and gives the whole community a chance at feedback. Moreover, the presentation itself will create some accountability on the part of the group to push through with their plans. Community presentation and validation of the plan is an important step at this stage of the process.

Tools for community planning and evaluation

1. Action planning – There are a number of models for making action plans. I have encouraged communities to keep it as simple as possible in the initial process and then have them expand and make more complex ones later on. Once they develop good skills of doing a basic action plan, they can move on to anything else they desire.

In our simple action plan, we go back to the Venn diagram and look at the resources needed to accomplish the project that in turn will solve the priority problem. Using the lack of water problem and spring development project as the solution, the community would come up with a plan that basically answers the following questions: what, who, when, how, and with?

A sample action plan for a village water system might look as follows:

Figure 17. A Simple Village Action Plan

WHAT	WHO	WHEN	HOW	WITH
① A plan/design drawn by the village	Juan and Diego	By next week	Survey and drawing w/ estimates	Local resources
② Present plan to all local villagers for approval	Sarah	April 15	Call a village meeting	Local resources
③ Take approved plan and request to district government	Village Development Committee	May 1 at District Meeting	Village head sets appointment	Leaders need money from treasurer - fare
④ Ask for technical help from outside to verify plan	Village head	May 1 at District Meeting	Present formal request in writing	Ask for govt. or NGO technician
⑤ Present revised plan to village	Sarah	Within 1 month of new design	Call a village meeting	Outside tech. makes present
⑥ Begin gathering local materials	Juan (In-charge)	Within 1 month of new design	Assign tasks to villager	Gather items locally
⑦ Begin gathering outside materials	Village Development Committee	Within 1 month of new design	Formal requests to govt. and NGO's	Local resources

The above plan takes the basic resources/actions needed as identified in the Venn diagram and places them under the "what" column. The community then fills out the other things that need to happen as to "who will do this action," "when does it need to be done," "how will it be done," and "with what resources will it need to be done." At the point of listing the "whats," I encourage the group to try and think chronologically such as not only "what" needs to happen but also what needs to happen first and so on. It is by no means a perfect planning tool but I have found it to be simple enough and effective for most groups.

2. Community covenants – Sometimes, a simple covenant or "promise" of the community by its members can be a powerful stim-

ulus for following through on a planned project. Depending on the local culture, a community can draft a covenant that they all agree to abide by in their efforts toward implementing a particular project or plan. The promise is made to themselves, the insiders, and not to us the outsiders. It can be verbal or, in most cases, written and displayed publicly in the community for all to see and refer to from time to time. Making a covenant is also a good window to sharing about covenants that God has made in His word.

3. Formalized MOAs/MOUs – Memorandums of Agreement or Memorandums of Understanding can be a more formal way of a community agreeing to a course of action. Again, while most MOAs/MOUs are not legally binding, they can be powerful reminders and encouragements to the community to continue in its agreed to development plan. A MOA/MOU usually consists of stating parties involved, expectations of the parties, conditions of the agreement for completion/termination, and signature/date lines by agreeing parties. A sample MOA can be found in Appendix 2 at the end of this book.

4. Community presentation – When the group develops a plan, many times, there are others in the community who have not been a part of the process. We encourage the public presentation and discussion of the plan. This reinforces the will of those involved to make sure the plan is carried out. It also can encourage others in the community to join in. They may have been skeptical or even felt alienated in the

process but now could join for a more encompassing community involvement.

5. Launching ceremony – After plans have been made and agreed upon, we also encourage a public launching ceremony to the plan/project decided upon. This would be a good time to invite local government officials and even religious leaders (depending upon the cultural context and appropriateness). It is an important way to give value to what the community has done and again reinforces the seriousness of following through with their project. This could be held in a public place like a government office or religious building. It also often involves the community serving snacks/food as they host people to view their proposed work.

6. Appointment of overseer/committee/head of project – In some cultures, there needs to be someone to oversee the whole project/plan and make sure things are accomplished. Again, whether you do this or not depends largely upon the local culture. However, an overseer that helps to keep things on schedule can be an effective tool for plan implementation. We prefer that this person be a non-paid community volunteer. This reinforces the fact that this is a community project that the community wants to accomplish for the benefit of the community.

Chapter Summary

- Our community development process and use of the tools is leading toward the community coming together and developing a plan of action to address initially one key problem in their community.

- A plan can help the community focus on next steps to accomplish a goal and gain valuable skills to address other issues in the future.

- Remember, we are not just doing a project. Our desire is to see the community come together, work together in unity, and gain new capabilities and capacities in order to sustainably meet their needs now and for the future.

Chapter 10
Step Five Tools: The Community Monitors, Evaluates, Celebrates, and Moves on to Next Problem

So, the plan has been created and is in place. It has been presented to the leaders. Now how does the community proceed, and how do they ensure that there is quality and timely action taking place according to their plan?

Tools for Community Monitoring and Evaluation

1. Monitoring and evaluation plan – At this stage, the group can choose an overseer from the community to "monitor" the project. Better yet, they can create an oversight committee to make sure the action plan is being implemented.

2. Regularly scheduled community progress meetings – Regular group meetings, started at the very beginning of this process, are the core elements in making sure that things are happening on schedule. The community should already be in the habit of meeting together and these regular meetings could serve as the forum for monitoring and evaluation. Also, spot-checks can be conducted by the committee members as well.

3. Goal and Progress (GAP) analysis – One tool we teach for this stage is called Gap analysis. This is a simple way of asking, "What was supposed to have been done, what has actually been done, and what is the gap that we need to close in order for the particular action to be accomplished?" Making a simple chart with those three headings and filling it out per major action on the community action plan can lead to the identification of needed measures to get the project back on track.

Figure 18. A Goal and Progress (GAP) Analysis

GOALS	NEEDED ACTION TO BE TAKEN...	PROGRESS
1. Plan drawn up	☆	Done
2. Present plan	☆	Done
3. Take plan to government	Need to get technical design for approval	Not done
4. Get design	Completed next week	In progress
5. Present plan to village	March 15 meeting	To do

4. Community celebration upon completion of project – When the community has achieved a particular goal or completed a project, do not forget to lead them into a time of celebration. This celebration does not have to be formal but should involve as much of the community as possible in order for all of the villagers to take credit and

celebrate their accomplishments. Many communities have never cele-brated success together and this would be a positive event to introduce to instill confidence for future projects. It also could be a good time for the leaders of the first project to address the core group in a chal-lenging way to begin working on other problems. At this celebration, they could post their situational maps, vision maps, and other tools and explain the process they went through to those who were not a part of the first group. In some cases, we have seen communities invite neighboring communities to join the celebration and used the time to introduce their community development process.

One key here for the development worker is to be a part of the celebration but not lead it. The victory belongs to the community and the credit needs to be reflected back to the community members who participated in the project. Also, a key role of the development worker at this stage is to encourage the community groups to move on to big-ger and better projects. He/she could help facilitate the process again but in a good development process, the local people should be taking more and more ownership as well as leadership and initiative in carry-ing out the village development meetings.

A Word About the Community Development Tools

As we wrap up the examples of tools for each stage of the commu-nity development process, I would like to share a few observations that we have learned regarding their use.

• The focus is not the tools – Sometimes, the temptation is to get caught up in using the tools. It is nice to have a great looking map, a snappy plan, etc., but we should remember that the tools are a vehicle to move us toward good community participation and interaction. We are not building "tools" but rather qualities such as community, confidence, and capacities. The tools are just tools.

• The tools are about visualizing and participating – We could ask the same questions that we are asking without using these tools. However, the tools actually help us to slow down and visualize what the community is feeling and experiencing. They also allow for and facilitate participation by the whole community.

• Meetings are one of the best tools – One of the most overlooked tools in the development process is the simple art of getting people to meet together. Meetings that are productive and result in people discussing their problems and finding ways to solve those problems are effective tools for community development. You will notice that in all the stages of the development process, we are having community meetings. You might say that the community meeting is the "center post" of the community development process.

• Use culturally appropriate tools – We have introduced several types of tools as well as specific tools in this chapter. There are many more community development tools available to development workers. No one tool is the right one for every situation. Also, it is important to be very careful to learn which tools are not only good ones for communication but culturally appropriate as well.

• Where possible, use locally available materials – In many of the tools described in this chapter, we have used paper, pen, and other materials the village may or may not have. We encourage our development workers in the field to be creative and use what the local people have available. This will make the exercise more real, reproducible, and put the people at ease (no new technologies!).

• The tools belong to the people; let them do it – We have a saying for development meetings that goes, "give the pen to the villager." In other words, during the meeting, our goal is to get the community members talking and participating. We should not be lecturing and showing them how to do the tools to the point we take over the meeting. Minimum yet clear instructions are usually enough to get them moving. Do not hesitate to let them struggle a little bit with the tools. It is a learning process after all.

• The tools are not scientific but rather more "perceptive" – We need to keep reminding ourselves that the results from these exercises are more perspective and perception than concrete data. The maps, the rankings, and the analyses are the reality that the local people see and may contradict our good logic. However, unless a decision/plan is obviously harmful or detrimental to the community, we should be open-minded and let the community run with their decisions. After all, it is their community, not ours.

• Take time using the tools. It is more about interaction and discovery than a product – The fun is in the journey. Many times, we development workers want to rush through and get to a finished product that we can point to and hang on a wall. Even the villagers themselves sometimes get caught up in the competition of finishing fast or with the best output. We need to slow down and realize that the process of using the tool tends to be more important than the resulting charts or plans. How people work together, how they listen to each other and how they learn to make more community-based decisions may be the most important by-products of using tools such as these.

• Be creative; no tool is perfect – As I said before, there are unlimited community development tools out there. Also, you can make up your own as you go. Many of the ones described in this chapter are some that we have learned from other organizations and changed to fit our particular needs/situation. No one tool is perfect. Have fun! Experiment!

• You do not have to use all the tools, and you may use one tool more than once – The tools discussed in this book are some of the more common ones we have used over the years. You do not have to use all of these (but you would have fun doing so!), and you may find that one tool is particularly useful prompting you to use it more than once. There is nothing wrong with this.

Finally, here are some practical tips to remember when using the tools:

1. Give the pen to the community members – What this means is that we do not need to draw the maps or enter much into the community discussion. We should be the facilitators of the process and in that, we should "give the pen" to the community by letting them conduct the exercises. It is their community and they should be leading the process.

2. Encourage active participation by all – Try to facilitate participation by the quiet, the old, the young, etc. Where culturally appropriate, facilitate the overlooked groups such as women and youth to have a voice in the process.

3. Carefully observe the hidden things going on while the group uses the tools – While you are letting the group take the lead, you should take note as to the dynamics of the group. Who are the power brokers in the group? Who are the "bullies" who always want their way? Which one is the quiet, silent one who has lots of wisdom to share? When it comes to decision time, does the group look to one or two people and then follow?

4. Focus on the process not the product – Remember that they

will eventually wind up with a product. It may be a school, a road, a water system, etc. We will celebrate any of these things along with the community. But we want to focus on the process of how they get to that particular project. Is it fair and just to the whole community? Is it something that is beneficial to all? Does the process get at building a better sense of community among the members?

5. Pray. Pray for God to show you every step of the way the things that He is doing in the hearts and lives of each member of the community and what would be the window of opportunity for you to speak truth to them.

Chapter Summary

• It is important that the community celebrates its success.

• It is also important that as the community completes its first cycle of community development that this process becomes their process, not ours.

• Also it is important to remember that the goal of community development is not the use of the tools, diagrams, and process. It is people working together and growing in a way that they can solve their problems today and develop skills and capacities to solve problems in the future.

Chapter 11
Kingdom Impact: The Integration of Community Development and Church Planting

There are a number of successful models and methods to help address the acute and chronic needs of people. Our response to people and their suffering, be it short term or long-term, is one way in which we can "participate" in making Christ known in the world. We respond to people in need because:

• The love of Christ compels us – Our passion for Him calls us to have compassion on others. Just as Christ has loved us and laid down His life for us, we should do the same for others. We seek to follow the example of our Savior: to touch people where they are hurting.

• The need of people moves us – If we are truly transformed creatures, we cannot ignore the need of others no matter if they are or are not a part of the body of Christ. We are to be like Jesus who, when He saw the crowds, "He felt compassion for them, because they were weary and worn out, like sheep without a shepherd." (Matthew 9:36)

• The mandates of the Bible command us – Over and over in the Scriptures, God commands His people to care for the poor and needy. He has a special place in His heart for the oppressed. He looks after the widow and orphan. He commands His people to have His same heart for the world.

• The desire to make Christ known in word and deed inspires us – We see relief and development ministries as genuine expressions of the gospel. Our heart to make Christ known in word and deed is given credence through our reaching out to those in their deepest hour of need.

In addition, our response to the poor and needy is an effective tool in seeing the gospel go forth. You may ask, "How?" I will answer this by sharing an evaluation tool we use with our teams in the field. When they are trying to assess whether they are making any progress in terms of Kingdom, I have the team do a self-evaluation. They ask themselves (first privately, and then collectively) if they are doing the following:

1. Are you really helping people and making a difference in their lives?

2. Are you praying without ceasing, praying as you go, and praying with and for the people with whom you are working?

3. Are you constantly looking to see where God is working in your people? And when you see it, are you joining Him in the work?

4. Are you living incarnationally among the people with whom you have been called to serve? Are you living out Jesus in their midst?

5. Are you incorporating God's values and Bible stories into every situation that comes up?

6. Are you intentionally sharing your faith and making disciples?

If any team or field worker can answer, "yes" to all or most of these questions, I would say to them that they should not worry because the results will follow. God's word and work will not return void.

Some Case Studies of the Integration of Relief and Development with Kingdom Impact

Returning to Dr. Fielding's "ABCs" of relief and development (health) strategies, I would like to share a few case studies of development projects that have shown how these items are fleshed out both in physical and spiritual results. These are taken from a recent short booklet that was put together by our relief and development team. I believe they serve as good examples, inspiration, and practical demonstration of how relief and development work integrates with a gospel and missions strategy.

Case Study #1:
FAITH Gardening and Church Planting, South Asia

Project Type: Agriculture, Food Security

Short Summary: In an area suspicious of outsiders, especially Christians, this project has allowed access to almost 160 villages. Over 1,600 people have been trained in gardening and most of them are seekers of truth in the gospel. There have been 233 baptisms from this project with 13 house churches being started in the last year.

Main Story: India has a predominantly agricultural-based economy, but agriculture is providing little revenue to most rural families. Many areas are also experiencing political turmoil, with radical militants having a strong presence in many rural pockets. This limits accessibility for those seeking to share the gospel, and also strains the ability of rural families to grow sufficient food for daily needs. Local partners have found a significant need of many who live in such areas is for knowledge and empowerment to grow sufficient vegetables for home use and income generation. While access for "traditional" evangelism is sharply controlled by local political groups, teams of agricultural trainers are welcomed into these remote political "hot-spots." Local teams of believers have introduced and provided training in proven FAITH (Food Always In The Home) gardening techniques that allows families to both maintain a sufficient year-round diet and move toward economic self-sufficiency.

Three years ago, the team started discipleship and church planting training to go along with the agriculture work. During that time they noted that while there was openness to the gospel, access was limited in more remote areas due to the restrictions of local political militants. In the following two years, national partners offered 14 FAITH Garden training seminars. They used this training as an entry strategy for evangelism and church planting, and they experienced an overwhelming response and openness to the gospel in every place they went to teach gardening. In one village seminar, 60 representatives came from 15 different remote villages to undergo the training. In all, 160 villages received FAITH Garden training, 166 FAITH Garden beds were prepared, 1,601 seekers are seeking to know more about Christ, 51 prayer cells have been started, 705 people are attending the prayer cells, 13 house churches have been started, and 233 people are attending house churches and have undergone baptism. FAITH Gardens are being planted, people are being encouraged by the produce that is being grown in the FAITH gardens, new FAITH garden teachers are being trained, numerous new prayer cells are being started, the Gospel is being preached, and people are starting to become Christ-followers.

ABCDE's

Access:

• Accessed gained to "closed" areas as local populations and local political control allows for training in the gardening techniques.

• Local authorities opposed to the gospel and suspicious of Christians are happy to receive the gardening training, and tolerant of the Good News being shared as a part of the gardening training time in villages.

Behind Closed Doors:

• During the multi-day training, direct access to village homes and public places is provided, and trainers utilize time of staying in the village to teach both gardening and the Good News of Christ.

• The gardening training includes a strong emphasis on how God is the provider of all things needed for our lives, and that we must live in right relation with him if we are to avail of the love and blessings he desires to share with us, and that this right relation comes through the grace given through Jesus' death and resurrection.

• Follow-up sessions are offered in separate evening sessions for those interested in hearing more about the Gospel.

Care for the Needy/Church Planting:

• 160 villages received training in how to feed their families.

• 1,601 seekers are seeking to know more about Christ.

• 51 prayer cells were started.

• 705 people are attending the prayer cells.

• 13 house churches have been started in past year.

Disciple-Making:

• Disciples are encouraged to grow in faith and are challenged to take the gospel message and valuable gardening practices to new villages within the state.

• There were 233 baptisms in the past year.

Empower the Church:

• Newly planted churches share the gardening, natural pesticide, fertilizers production, and seed preserving techniques in new villages. Following the pattern they have seen, new believers also allocate specific time for further gospel sharing in the new areas they go, and among family, friends, and neighbors.

Case Study #2:
Community Health Interventions in Southeast Asia

Project Type: Health Care Education

Short Summary: This is a simple health care project aimed at health education in needy rural Southeast Asian villages. Seventeen (17) villages have been accessed with 1,100 people trained in basic health care. 64 believers have resulted from this work with a total of 13 Bible studies starting resulting in six churches.

Main Story: This community health project came about because of the great physical needs seen in village life. Cambodia is a country with very few medical treatment options for its people. During the reign of the Khmer Rouge, most professional people were put to death in a genocide and it has taken a long time for the country to recover. Thus, the main points of this project are teaching the use of herbal medicines/health interventions and the training of local women to train their peers about good health practices and nutrition at the village level. This project is about transforming villages. It began years ago as several people saw the need and had broken hearts every time they stepped foot in these poor villages. Instead of being overwhelmed by the poverty and throwing their hands up, they created this project. Basically, they saw a need and were compelled to find a way to intervene without creating dependency. The key to this project has been the people being sent out. All workers are discipled and trained in traditional medicine, pregnancy care, hygiene, and health and have experience in seeing radically changed villages.

In the second year of the project, they have doubled the number of people taught and expanded their area of coverage. For the past nine months, they have taught in 17 villages with a total of 1,110 learners. The most exciting part is that they have many volunteers for the first time that go with them and share their faith while physical needs are being met. Because of this, results are better than ever as they have seen greater impact on health and beliefs. The local volunteers come from the villages that were taught the year before. These volunteers have brought excitement to each location and validate both the health and faith messages shared. Each of the 17 villages has seen large numbers of those who have changed their health behaviors, increased consumption of more nutritious foods, had immediate health needs met, and have seen many find faith in Christ. Within nine months, the workers have facilitated the visit of 529 poor and pregnant ladies from rural areas to their local health centers. This has allowed the delivery of their babies in a safe environment that provides prenatal care, vitamins, and immunizations for mother and baby. Moreover, they were able to assist 310 people to access clinics and hospitals in a nearby city where they received treatment often including surgery or even chemotherapy. 300 or more were treated in their homes by the home-to-home visiting team and village health groups.

This year, through this amazing outreach of love, the project has seen 64 people baptized, 13 Bible study groups begun, and six churches started within the first nine months! The Spirit of God is moving in each of these locations and even calling out volunteers to accompany the project staff to the next places. The key to the success has been the national laborers on this project. They have truly learned to love their neighbor as themselves and to overcome all obstacles to help those chained in poverty. They bravely enter these villages that overwhelmed normal people and gradually help all the villagers in need. At the same time they boldly share their faith and disciple the many who believe.

ABCDE's

Access:

• 17 villages were opened up with 1,110 people participating in the program.

Behind Closed Doors:

• Training of leaders led to relationships allowing us to have deeper access to the people and communities.

Care/Church Planting:

• 64 people were baptized.

• Six churches were started out of this project.

Disciple-Making:

• 13 new Bible study groups were started.

Empower the Church:

• Holistic ministry such as this project allows local believers a natural bridge to others in need.

Case Study #3:
Craft Business Initiative, Central America

Project Type: Microenterprise/business

Short Summary: This project provided skills training and materials to ladies wanting to start a sewing business. Over 20 ladies have been trained and are now making modest but good incomes for their families. Over 100 people have heard the gospel with 10 making professions of faith and two new Bible studies and one church being started.

Main Story: In a poor neighborhood where there is violence and gangs, there are many families who are struggling to have food to eat. Many of the women are single mothers and tend to lock their children in the house so that they can sell something in order for the family to be able to buy food. There are at times small children (four-year-olds) taking care of their younger brothers and sisters. Teaching the women to make handicrafts in their homes while others can work at a location with child care would help them to have money to buy food as well as care for their children. The goal for this project has been to help families and to transform the neighborhood by providing work that would help all in the community. The women who started the work are the future teachers for new ladies that will be added as the business increases. The women themselves choose the area of handicraft they want to work in. Some are learning new skills of using sewing machines. The women have to work at a specified location (e.g. a skills training center) because of the need to keep machines in running order.

Within the first year, this project has become self-sustaining and able to support a second and third group of women to be trained and employed. In the community, more of the older children are now able to go to school due to the increased income. The women are paid in local currency and have classes on money management as well.

A work place has been rented for house equipment and supplies and to allow for a clean and safe place to work. The house is located across the street from where the women live, so transportation is not an issue. A store in the downtown historical district was donated to the project in order to use to sell their products. The store was opened October 30, 2011 with a grand opening and prayer time. The business now has 20 women working and approximately 60 people benefitting from this project.

The local government liked how the project was working and offered some help for the women as well. The government permitted them to participate in the annual Christmas bazaar. New women have been recruited into the group and have begun making new products. The group has also begun collecting used clothes to sell in front of the workshop. The women have begun to train other women in crafts projects and how to work. The project has received some attention from others and staff were invited to speak on a radio/TV program. The segment was popular and the staff were invited back to give monthly updates on what was happening with the business. This actually helped the sales and gave them new contacts in the community.

This large neighborhood had been closed to the Gospel but now is open. Other areas nearby have become interested as well after hearing about the project.

ABCDE's

Access:

• A closed, dangerous community has been opened to the gospel.

• The local government has not only blessed but put resources into the project.

• Trained women are training others.

Behind Closed Doors:

• Relationships have been developed to allow sharing in homes that are a more neutral setting.

Care of Needy/Church Planting:

• A real need of widows/single moms has been addressed (income generation).

• Over 100 people have heard the gospel with 10 professing faith.

• One church has started as a result.

Disciple-Making:

• Two Bible studies have started as a result of this project.

Empower the Church:

• Women are now reaching/helping other women in the community.

Chapter Summary

• Our response to people and their suffering, be it short term or long-term, is one way in which we can "participate" in making Christ known in the world.

• Our heart and purpose for community development is to make Christ known in word and in deed. Thus, we call it "Kingdom" development.

Conclusion

There is still much to be said and discussed about community development that leads to a Kingdom impact. However, we have come to the end of this book and the best discussion will occur when you and I begin trying to apply the methods and processes that we have documented here. We are constantly hearing and learning from field practitioners what does and doesn't work. And we are continually gleaning new lessons and stories as well.

As we come to the end, I do want to remind us all that development for the sake of development is a good thing, but government and non-government agencies can do it as well or better than you and I can. The main difference in what we strive to achieve is development with a physical as well as a spiritual impact. Simply stated, we seek Kingdom impact through community development.

As you plan to venture into a community development strategy in your missions endeavor, I would encourage you to keep these few things in mind:

1. Is this approach central and crucial to your strategy for reaching your target group? In short, is a community development approach

strategic for your situation and your ultimate goals? Does your target group really need and are they interested in development for their local community?

2. Is there intentionality for gospel proclamation, church planting, and multiplication built into your overall plan? Assuming that "doing" community development will lead to church planting or a church planting movement is a false assumption.

3. Is there a methodology that you have chosen, learned, and are practicing to make sure that evangelism, church planting, and multiplication are facilitated throughout the community development process? It can be chronological storying (CBST), Training for Trainers (T4T), or one of several other methods, but what have you/your team chosen as the methodology for proclamation and multiplication?

4. Is what you are doing really helping people, both physically and spiritually? Are you making Christ known both in word and in deed? Is it a quality approach/program that truly helps people whether or not they come to faith? If it is worth doing, it is worth doing well. We should offer not only a testimony in words but a testimony in action.

Finally, I have a last set of reminders to share with you as I close.

1. Community development is not the perfect tool for missions. It

is one tool of many in the tool belt of your missions strategy. It is not for everyone to use. The host/target people group or population segment may not dictate the use of a community development approach. They may not need it and hence make the approach non-applicable in certain cases. In addition, you may not have the gifting, skills, and even calling to use this strategy. Furthermore, you and your team may not have the resources to attempt this approach. (I am not only talking about financial resources here but expertise, vision, etc.). In short, the method and strategy of community development approaches to missions is not for everyone.

2. There is growing evidence that community development is a valid approach and strategy for missions if done correctly. We are seeing a growing number of people groups being accessed, helped, and churches planted with each passing day. All of this is being done through a community development approach. Again, we are not saying that it is a perfect tool, but it is a valid one and the growing evidence is overwhelming and cannot be ignored.

3. The lack of urban models is something that needs to be addressed. I do not apologize for my lack of experience in the urban setting. Rural work is mainly what I have done and who I am. I am looking forward to seeing more urban models of community development emerge. We are seeing a few. However, I think in the future, we will see more and they in turn will help us learn how to do Kingdom

focused community development better in those environs.

4. The best community development strategies and programs are those that empower national partners. This is probably not surprising to most of our readers. However, even though it is obvious, it bears stating. Our most precious resource for the work is not our money, education, or status. It is the partners that we have all over the world who are from and in the very communities we are seeking to reach. They have the language and culture and the ability to enter, implement, share, proclaim, and demonstrate the gospel in ways so much better than we do as outsiders. Moreover, the best case studies and results that we see for total Kingdom impact mostly come from those projects and programs that are being led by our national partners.

5. Most of what is described here is for the overseas practitioner, but the local church in the United States and other places can use a community development strategy for missions. There are some adjustments to be made to the process described in this book when a church in the USA decides to take a community development missions approach. As we work and partner with churches here and other places, we are learning new things. However, that is a topic for another time.

Community Development: From Here to Eternity

A wise man once asked me a very thought provoking question …

"How do you really help a person?"

In other words, how do you help them in a way that really helps? That does not hurt them in the long run? How do you help them in a way that preserves dignity and empowers them to move on in self-sufficiency and self-determination? In short, how to you truly help a person?

It is a hard question to answer.

One thing I know is that there are a few keys. First, we need to start by trying to understand that person and their situation before making our thoughts and agendas known. The priority needs to be on the person and their needs, thoughts, and dreams, not ours.

Second, whatever we do, it should be done in a way that does not just help an individual but also takes into consideration that the individual is a part of a greater community. It may be as small as a family unit. It may be a village community or even a larger one. But I have never known anyone who lives in a vacuum.

Third, we need to see them and their community as eternal beings and not just temporal ones. C. S. Lewis says that you and I have never met a mere mortal. We all are eternal beings. As we look at helping people with their struggles in hunger, poverty, poor health, etc., we need to keep in mind that the greatest need of any person is to be reconciled to God their Creator through Jesus Christ, His Son.

So when we endeavor to help people through community development that in reality creates an avenue for Kingdom impact, we need to remember that we are helping people from here to eternity.

References and Resources for Further Reading

BOOK RESOURCES

General Missions

Hiebert, Paul G. and Meneses, Eloise Hiebert. 1995. *Incarnational Ministry: Planting Churches in Band, Tribal, Peasant and Urban Societies.* Baker Books, Grand Rapids, Michigan.

Myers, Bryant L. 1993. *The Changing Shape of World Missions.* MARC Publications, Monrovia, California.

History of Southern Baptists Human Needs Ministries

Crawley, Winston. 1985. *Global Mission: A Story to Tell.* Broadman Press, Nashville, TN.

Christians and Hunger; Hunger Issues

Brown, Lester R. 1996. *Tough Choices: Facing the Challenge of Food Scarcity.* The Worldwatch Environment Alert Series. W. W. Norton Company, New York.

Parham, Robert. 1988. *What Shall we do in a Hungry World?* New Hope Publications, Birmingham, Alabama.

Sine, Tom. 1981. *The Mustard Seed Conspiracy.* Word Publishing, Waco, Texas

Stearns, Richard. 2009. *The Hole in our Gospel.* Thomas Nelson Publishers, Nashville, TN. 303 pgs.

Missions and Development

Bradshaw, Bruce. 1993. *Bridging the Gap: Evangelism, Development and Shalom.* MARC Publications, Monrovia, California.

Cheyne, John R. 1996. *Incarnational Agents: A Guide to Developmental Ministry.* New Hope, Birmingham, Alabama.

Corbett, Steve and Brian Fikkert. 2009. *When Helping Hurts: How to Alleviate Poverty without Hurting the Poor.* Moody Publishers, Chicago, Illinois.

DeYoung, Kevin and Gilbert, Greg. 2011. *What is the Mission of the Church: Making Sense of Social Justice, Shalom and the Great Commission.* Crossway, Wheaton, IL, USA.

Dyrness, William A. 1983. *Let the Earth Rejoice!: A Biblical Theology of Holistic Mission.* Fuller Seminary Press, Pasadena, California.

Greenway, Roger S. 1998. *Together Again: Kinship of Word and Deed.* MARC Publications, Monrovia, California.

Lupton, Robert. 2011. Toxic Charity: *How Churches and Charities Hurt Those They Help – and How to Reverse It.* HarperOne Publishing, New York, New York.

Lupton, Robert. 2007. *Compassion, Justice and the Christian Life: Rethinking Ministry to the Poor.* Regal Books, Ventura, CA, USA.

McAlpine, Thomas H. 1995. *By Word, Work and Wonder.* MARC Publications, Monrovia, California.

Myers, Bryant L. 1999. *Walking With the Poor: Principles and Practices of Transformational Development.* Orbis Books, Maryknoll, New York.

Myers, Bryant L., Ed. 1999. *Working With the Poor: New Insights and Learnings from Development Practitioners.* MARC Publications, Monrovia, California.

O'Gorman, Frances. 1992. *Charity and Change: From Bandaid to Beacon.* World Vision, Australia.

Palmer, J. Jeffrey. 2004. *Kingdom Development: A Passion for Souls and a Compassion for People.* ACTS Co. Ltd., Chiang Mai, Thailand.

Palmer, J. Jeffrey. 2005. *Poverty and the Kingdom of God: What in the World is God Doing About the Poor?* ACTS Co. Ltd., Chiang Mai, Thailand.

Palmer, J. Jeffrey. 2007. *Kingdom Communities: Koinonea as if it Really Mattered.* ACTS Co. Ltd., Chiang Mai, Thailand.

Platt, David. 2015. *Counter Culture: A Compassionate Call to Counter Culture in a World of Poverty, Same-Sex Marriage, Racism, Sex Slavery, Immigration, Abortion, Persecution, Orphans and Pornography.* Tyndale House Publishers, Nashville, TN.

Ram, Eric, Editor. 1995. *Transforming Health: Christian Approaches to Healing and Wholeness.* MARC Publications, Monrovia, California.

Yamamori, Tetsunao, Myers, B. L., and Conner, D., Editors, 1995. *Serving With the Poor in Asia.* MARC Publications, Monrovia, California.

Participatory Methods

Chambers, Robert. 1997. *Whose Reality Counts: Putting the First Last.* ITDG Publishing, South Hampton Row, London.

Chambers, Robert. 2002. *Participatory Workshops: A Sourcebook of 21 Sets of Ideas and Activities.* Earthscan Publications, London.

Cooke, Bill and Kothari, Uma, Editors. 2001. *Participation: The New Tyranny?* Zed Books Ltd., London.

Hope, Ann and Timmel, Sally. 1999. *Training for Transformation: A Handbook for Community Workers*. ITDG Publishing, London.

Horne, Peter M. and Stur, Werner W. 2003. *Developing Agricultural Solutions with Smallholder farmers – How to get Started with Participatory Approaches*. ACIAR Monograph No. 99, Canberra, Australia.

Kumar, Somesh. 2002. *Methods for Community Participation: A Complete Guide for Practitioners*. ITDG Publishing, London.

Pretty, Jules N. 1995. *Regenerating Agriculture: Policies and Practice for Sustainability and Self-Reliance*. Earthscan Publications Ltd., London.

General Development

Bolton, Giles. 2006. *Aid and Other Dirty Business: How Good Intentions have Failed the World's Poor*. Ebury Press, London.

Collier, Paul. 2007. *The Bottom Billion: Why the Poorest Countries are Failing and What Can Be Done About It*. Oxford University Press, London.

Diamond, Jared. 1997. *Guns, Germs and Steel: A Short History of Everbody for the Last 13,000 Years*. Vintage House Publishing, London.

Diamond, Jared. 2005. Collapse: *How Societies Choose to Fail or Survive*. Penguin Books Ltd., London.

Easterly, William. 2006. *The White Man's Burden*. Oxford University Press, London.

Friedman, Thomas L. 2005. *The World is Flat: A Brief History of the Twenty-First Century*. Farrar, Straus and Giroux, New York.

Gladwell, Malcolm. 2000. *The Tipping Point: How Little Things can make a Big Difference.* Abacus Press, London.

Harrison, Lawrence E. 2000 (Updated Edition). *Underdevelopment is a State of Mind.* Madison Books, New York.

Polak, Paul. Out of Poverty: *What Works When Traditional Approaches Fail.* Berrett-Koehler Publishers, San Francisco, CA.

Sachs, Jeffrey. 2005. *The End of Poverty: How We can make it Happen in our Lifetime.* Penguin Books Ltd., London.

Sachs, Jeffrey. 2008. *Common Wealth: Economics for a Crowded Planet.* Penguin Books Ltd., USA.

Shumacher, E. F. 1973. *Small is Beautiful: Economics as if People Mattered.* Harper and Row Publishers, Inc., New York.

Christians and Environment; General Environment

Bear, Firman E. 1986. *Earth: The Stuff of Life.* University of Oklahoma Press, Norman.

McDonough, Sean. *To Care for the Earth.* (Out of Print) Published in the Philippines (based upon McDonough's experience among the T'boli of the southern Philippines.)

Roberts, W. Dayton. *Patching God's Garment: Environment and Mission in the 21st Century.* 1994. MARC Publications, Monrovia, California.

WEB RESOURCES

Community Development

www.chalmers.org. – The Chalmers Center at Covenant College. This is a great website/organization for beginning learners regarding community development. They offer on-line courses, resources and webinars dealing with development issues, microfinance, etc.

www.gobgr.org – This is the Baptist Global Response website. It will give basic information about projects around the world and contact information on how to get involved. There are a number of free downloadable resources as well on the resource page.

www.ideorg.org – This is International Development Enterprise's website and link to Paul Polak's work. Paul is a down-to-earth technology buff that likes to see practical solutions for problems. A lot of good ideas here.

www.marcpublications.com – This is World Vision International's publications website. The materials on this website are to be purchased but they have some excellent resources available.

www.tilz/tearfund.org – This is Tear Fund's publications and learning zone. It is the home of one of the best community development resource publications available, namely the Footsteps newsletter. The publications page has a user-friendly search engine built in to give easy access to any topic covered.

www.echonet.org - ECHO is a great agriculture resources website. ECHO is a Christian organization out of Ft. Myers, Florida helping to provide resources and information about appropriate agriculture technologies.

www.planotes.org - This is a site of the International Institute of Environment and Development. It is a source of the Participatory Learning and Action (PLA) Notes. A very helpful source of CD tools.

Microfinance/Microenterprise Development

www.kiva.org - Kiva is an organization that links potential donors with the poor of the world needing cash/loans to begin small businesses. Sort of an "eBay" of microfinance linking the "haves" with the "have nots."

www.microplace.com - An investment website where your investments help provide cash flows to the poor.

General Information

www.globalissues.org - A good general information site on environment, poverty, health, education, etc. Looks at problems from a global perspective and is well documented.

www.un.org/en/globalissues - This is the UN's website dealing with global issues. It is very deep and leads to multiple links to UN agencies, global information, etc.

Disaster Relief

http://www.usaid.gov/our_work/humanitarian_assistance/ disaster_assistance/resources/pdf/fog_v3.pdf - This is a general but comprehensive guide to give a basic idea of what disasters are and how to form a response to them.

http://reliefweb.int - The "go to" place for global disaster information.

Appendix 1
A Sample Community Development Process in a Central Asian Community

Appendix 1 is a memorandum of understanding (translated from the local language) that all of the representatives of the village and our office signed at the beginning of the second meeting. There are around 400 families in the village, but only about 120 actual homes. What you have are multiple families sharing a yard or large extended families in one yard. The head of our community has 22 children (with two wives) himself – with many of those still living at home. We have roughly one representative for every five or six homes, so we've had around twenty guys participating in the CDP meetings.

We were a bit worried that participation would dwindle as the meetings progressed, but we've had good attendance at all meetings. One of the more regular on-time (unusual for this culture) attendees is one who we're not sure still fully understands the process and often questions why we're doing what we're doing, but he is still faithful to come. Here's a breakdown of the meetings we've had so far and some difficulties and breakthroughs:

Second Meeting (Goal: Awareness)

a. Participants weren't prepared for what we told them to expect at this meeting (i.e. preparing a map of the community or working on a timeline).

b. Had a hard time understanding why this was so important (i.e. can't we just give you a list of projects?).

c. Most of the participants have a bleak outlook on the future of this country, so it was hard for them to envision anything in the future. Questions like "How do you see the food situation in 10 years?" had to be predicated with "assuming security is good".

d. Most realized they weren't as prepared as they should have been for this meeting and made plans to get together with other members of the community and with each other before the next meeting for information sharing.

Third Meeting (Goal: Problem Identification)

a. The vision mapping was very interesting, though it took them awhile to start thinking outside the box. Once they understood the goal of the exercise they began to get creative. Fun times.

b. Listed many problems that seemed to be genuine and legitimate concerns.

Fourth Meeting (Goal: Problem Analysis)

a. Should have probably introduced a sample problem tree at the previous meeting. It again took the group a while to get used to the exercise, but once again moved quickly once they understood the value of the task.

b. I was encouraged this meeting to see everyone valuing the opinions of others. We had one older man who doesn't say much in the meetings, but spoke up in this meeting. While his statement was relevant at that particular moment, the group made sure to come back and add his input to the problem tree when it came time.

This is what we've accomplished so far. The group has been moving fairly quickly through the process and are anxious to see what will develop.

As we meet it would seem the group is moving toward a "septic" or drainage system for the community. This seems to have come to the forefront and meets several of the identified needs/problems of the community (i.e. poor health of children, tainted water, bad smell outside, etc.). We'll see what develops in coming meetings – we've got another one tonight.

All in all I think the process is going well. For many of the participants this is the first time they've heard, much less worked, through such a systematic process.

I think it is opening many minds and challenging people to think more like a community. It is certainly local-style, with much flair and passionate speaking, but still accomplishing the goals we've set and moving the village in the right direction.

Fifth Meeting (Solution Identification)

a. As a group we went back and reviewed some of the problem

trees from last time. There were some new ideas or additions, which was good to see that people were thinking on these things outside of our actual meeting times.

b. The group worked very methodically through the process of choosing a problem to tackle. There were varying opinions, but everyone was heard and allowed time to defend their position.

c. It was interesting to see how the solution (or project) they chose met several of the root problems that they mentioned across several problem trees. I wasn't sure where they were going to go with things for a while, but as solutions to problems were discussed, this one kept coming to the forefront.

d. The community identified a septic system (in reality more of a cesspit system) as the number one solution for the top problem (unhealthy water). Again, this solution actually helps many of the problem areas they identified (poor health of children, tainted water, bad smell outside, etc.).

e. The Venn Diagram activity was amazing. The first time through every responsibility of the project/solution ended up outside the circle! After a brief thought, our community mobilizer said, "Isn't this community development? What part is the community doing?" The second time through it was if someone had turned on the light. People began to see that the community could contribute (quite a bit actually). At the end someone made the comment that "at first we thought we could do nothing, but now we see that we can contribute." I made sure that he said that loud enough for everyone to hear.

Sixth Meeting (Planning)

a. I think the mood was "now we are getting to the good stuff – an action plan."

I wasn't sure how this one was going to go. My fear was we'd come out of this meeting with a list of things that our office was going to have to do. To my amazement I came out asking, "What do WE actually need to do?"

b. The community had taken charge and was moving the plan along. Our office would primarily be waiting on and encouraging the community as needed.

c. An interesting conversation happened during the course of this meeting. One of the elders spoke up halfway through the meeting and said something to the effect of "I'm not sure we should do this project." I thought, oh man, the whole process is about to be derailed. I was surprised to see others listen to his opinion, but then walk him back through the process and communicate to him that these concerns should have been voiced during a previous stage of the process and not now. They did this in a respectful and non-threatening manner and he soon admitted that yes, his comments would have been better suited to an earlier stage in the process and that he would remember this next time.

After our sixth and final "official" meeting the community began to carry out their responsibilities and are moving forward with their idea. They met as a greater community and announced the idea so that everyone was aware and onboard. They have been working through engineers and skilled laborers to come up with a budget and give us some estimate as to the amount of materials that will be needed. The community itself will be providing all non-skilled labor, tools (shovels, picks, wheelbarrows), and securing permission from the government. They will also choose the best sites for the cesspits and calculate the number of homes and lengths of pipe that will be needed. Frankly, they're doing all the legwork at this point and it's exciting to see.

Appendix 2
A Sample Memorandum of Understanding/Agreement

Memorandum of Understanding (MOU)

Between

Representatives of _____ (**Community "Insiders"**)

And

_____(**NGO, PO, Etc. "Outsider"**)

For

Initiation of the Community Development Process

in _____(**Name of community**)

Preamble:

In the name of the Mighty God, the representatives of _____ (**Name of community**) sign this MOU with _____(**NGO, PO, Etc. "Outsider"**) to signify the initiation of the community development process in _____(**Name of community**). Both _____ (**NGO, PO, Etc. "Outsider"**) and the representatives of _____ (**Name of community**) understand that the future of our community relies on our ability to better ourselves and meet the needs of our community through our own power and resources. This MOU pertains only to the process of community development and not to any particular project.

This MOU defines the rules and responsibility of both parties:

_____ (**NGO, PO, Etc. "Outsider"**) Obligations:

1. _____ (**NGO, PO, Etc. "Outsider"**) agrees to work with the representatives, and in essence the community, to instruct and guide them through the community development process.

2. At which point the community development process yields a viable solution to a problem identified by the members of _____ **(Name of community)**, _____ **(NGO, PO, Etc. "Outsider")** will partner with the community to work as an advocate to seek resources which are unobtainable from the local community.

3. _____ **(NGO, PO, Etc. "Outsider")** will not seek to impose its own agenda or ideas for potential problems or solutions, but will rely solely on the leadership of _____ **(Name of community)** to identify these needs and solutions via the community development process.

Representatives' of _____ **(Name of community)**. Obligations:

1. Representatives from the local community will do their best to reflect the concerns, needs, and ideas of all members of _____**(Name of community)** (young, old, women, men).

2. The representatives of _____**(Name of community)** will understand and work through the entire community development process.

3. The representatives of _____ **(Name of community)** will attend all meetings and work peacefully with one another in an atmosphere of honesty and cooperation.

We the undersigned pledge to uphold this MOU and work toward a better future for the community of _____ **(Name of community).**

Appendix 3
Notes on Community Surveys – Adapted from John Cheyne

Introduction – Each developmental/transformational project or program is different. Adaptations and changes may have to be made in consideration of local circumstances and cultural differences but the following are general considerations for gathering information in formulating your project/program.

Background Study – There should be a general description of the target area for the proposed project, including a complete picture of the community situation. Project managers need to clearly understand the economic, social, cultural, linguistic, ethnic, and religious aspects. Investigation should be made into the nature and types of problems that create need.

Sources of Information:

1. The community members

2. Existing government, voluntary relief and development agencies working in the area

3. Professionals in the area of low-income development

4. The body

5. Demographic studies/histories and records related to the area

6. Municipal, community or other national government offices

7. Community survey and/or (more preferably) PRA/PLA exercises

General Objectives of the Project Researchers:

1. To provide a valid sociological, demographic and statistical base

2. To provide the instruments necessary for carrying out the most effective and efficient approach toward meeting the needs of the target group in a holistic manner

3. Introduction of self and program into the community

4. Creating a filter that allows access to every family/home in the community. This filter will help determine initial participants based on interest, response and participation.

Community Survey Components:

1. Demographics and history/nature of the community …

* Family unit: size, type, sex, age, marital status, births, etc.

* Migration: from where? Why? Length of stay, planned duration, ties to rural area/urban area …

2. The Physical Environment

* Housing: type, condition, ownership, felt needs

* Clothing: quantity, conditions, felt needs

* Water: source, storage, felt needs

* Fuel: source, type, felt needs

* Food: source, diet, felt needs

* Refuse: disposal, toilet facilities, felt needs

* Bedding: furniture, blankets, felt needs

* Amenities: radios, TV, utensils, bicycles, other transport, etc.

3. The Psycho-Socioeconomic Environment:

* Education/literacy: School completion, vocational training, literacy skills

* Employment: occupation, type of employment, permanency

* Social: entertainment, memberships, social networks, leisure time

* Money: income, usage, borrowing

* Aspirations/changes: education, employment, social, money

4. The General Health

* Nutrition: adult/child consumption, approximate caloric intake per person (adult/child), preferences, infant feeding practices, etc.

* Sickness: kinds, treatment, causes, preventive measures, felt needs

5. The Community's Development Program

* Health and nutrition: awareness, participation, attitudes

* Family Planning: awareness, participation, attitudes, preferences

* Education/training: awareness, participation, attitudes, preferences

* Social: awareness, participation, attitudes, preferences

6. The Spiritual Situation

* Religion: What? How long? What level of involvement?

* Knowledge and values: life, death, God, Christ, the Bible

* Christian practices

* Traditional/religious practices

Research Permission: This is required in every place. You will need permission from the top down (government) and the bottom up (the people themselves). To try and undertake this kind of intensive research without proper permission is counterproductive and counter-intuitive to your plans.

gobgr.org

BAPTIST GLOBAL RESPONSE

HOW CAN BGR
HELP YOU?

- Resources
- Training
- Giving
- Volunteering

Stay tuned for Jeff Palmer's next book, *So You Want to Dig a Well in Africa?*